Life's a Picnic

A GRAYSCALE ADULT COLORING BOOK

**Fancy finger foods. A bottle of vino. Breathtaking scenery.
There's no denying that picnics are magical.**

Whether you're dreaming of a solo sandwich by the sea, a romantic feast under the stars with the one you love, or a leisurely lakeside lunch with friends, *Life's a Picnic* has the perfect coloring page to inspire your outdoor adventures.

These grayscale images are designed to stimulate your creativity, improve your fine motor skills, and induce a state of calm meditative focus.

Fine tip markers, colored pencils and watercolor mediums are all ideal for bringing these pages to life.

I0482420

COLORING IN GRAYSCALE: THE BASICS

COLORS

The existing shading on grayscale pages creates a beautiful, rich color palette when blended with multiple shades of the same color. Using multiple variations of blue, green, yellow, etc. will allow you to create a more lifelike final image.

MATERIALS

Colored pencils, watercolor pencils, blendable markers and crayons all work well for grayscale coloring. Use gel pens, fine tipped markers to enhance detail, and a watercolor brush or sponge for better blending technique.

BLENDING WITH GRAYSCALE

Try coloring over the darker gray areas with your darkest color shades for greater depth and saturation.

HAVE FUN

There is no wrong way to color. Just do what feels right!

CONNECT WITH US

We love seeing all the gorgeous works of art created with our grayscale coloring books. Post photos of your finished pages with your Amazon review, tweet at @HartGrayscale, or share them in the Grayscale Coloring Group on Facebook!

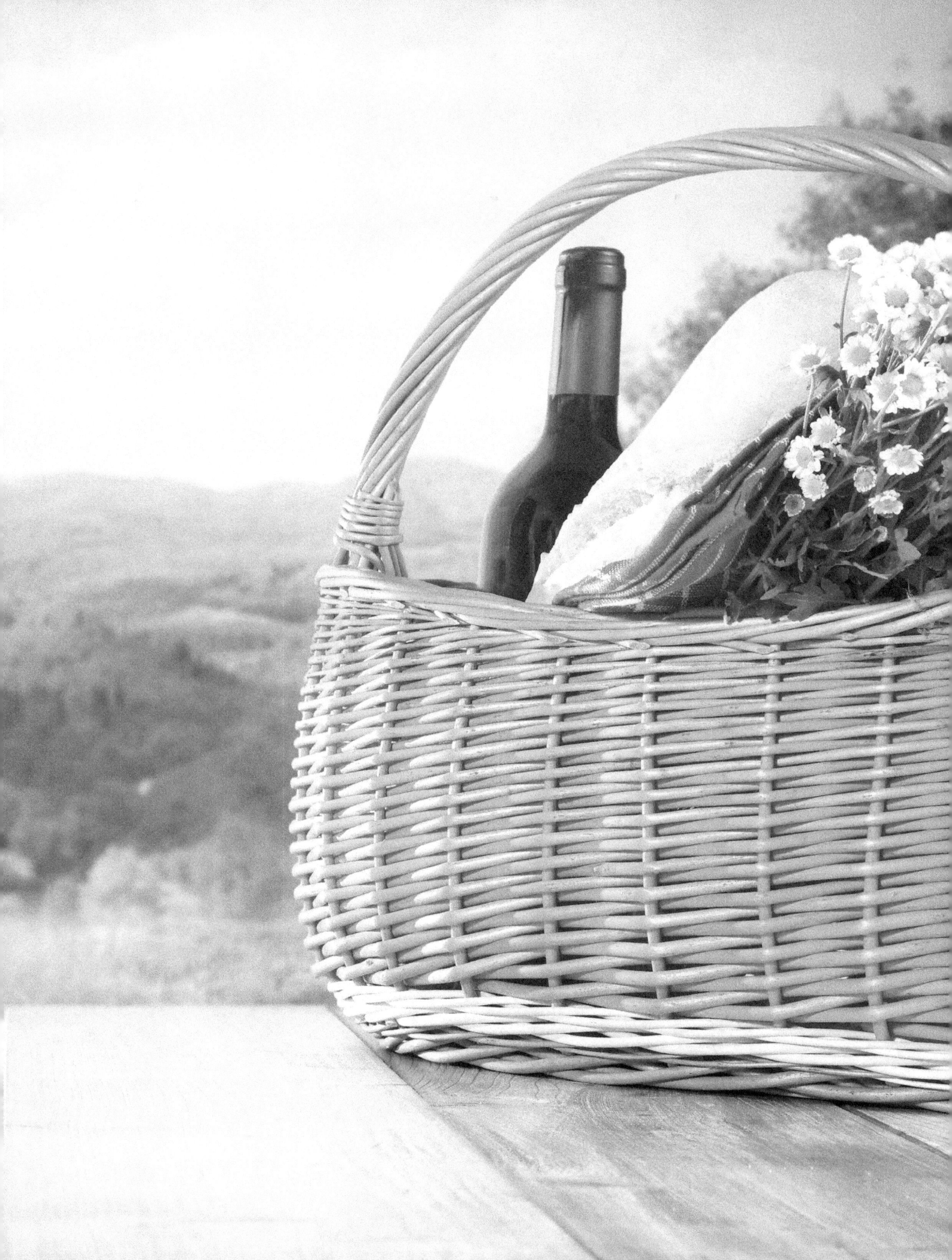

Materials Used:

Colored By:

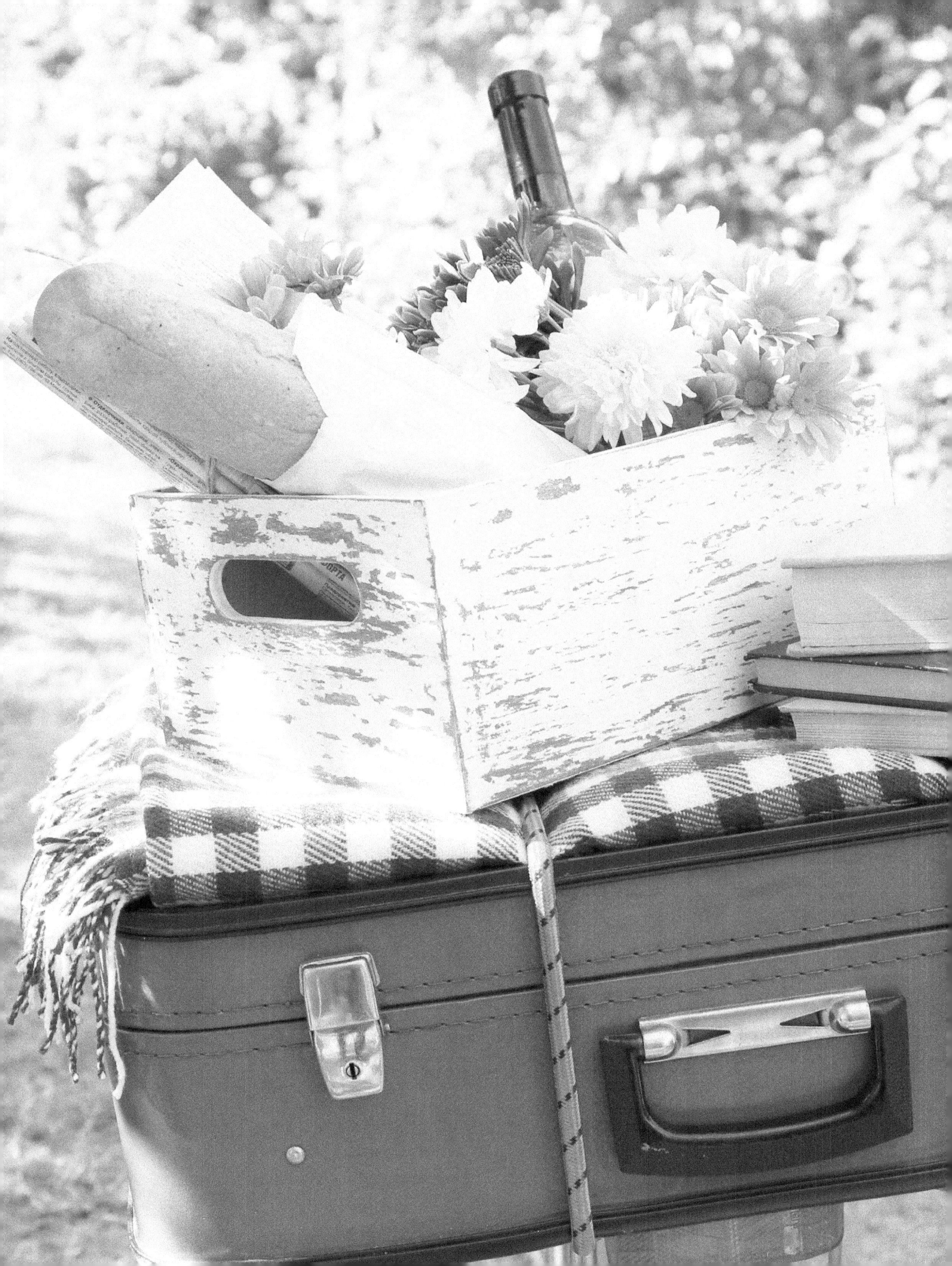

Materials Used:

Colored By:

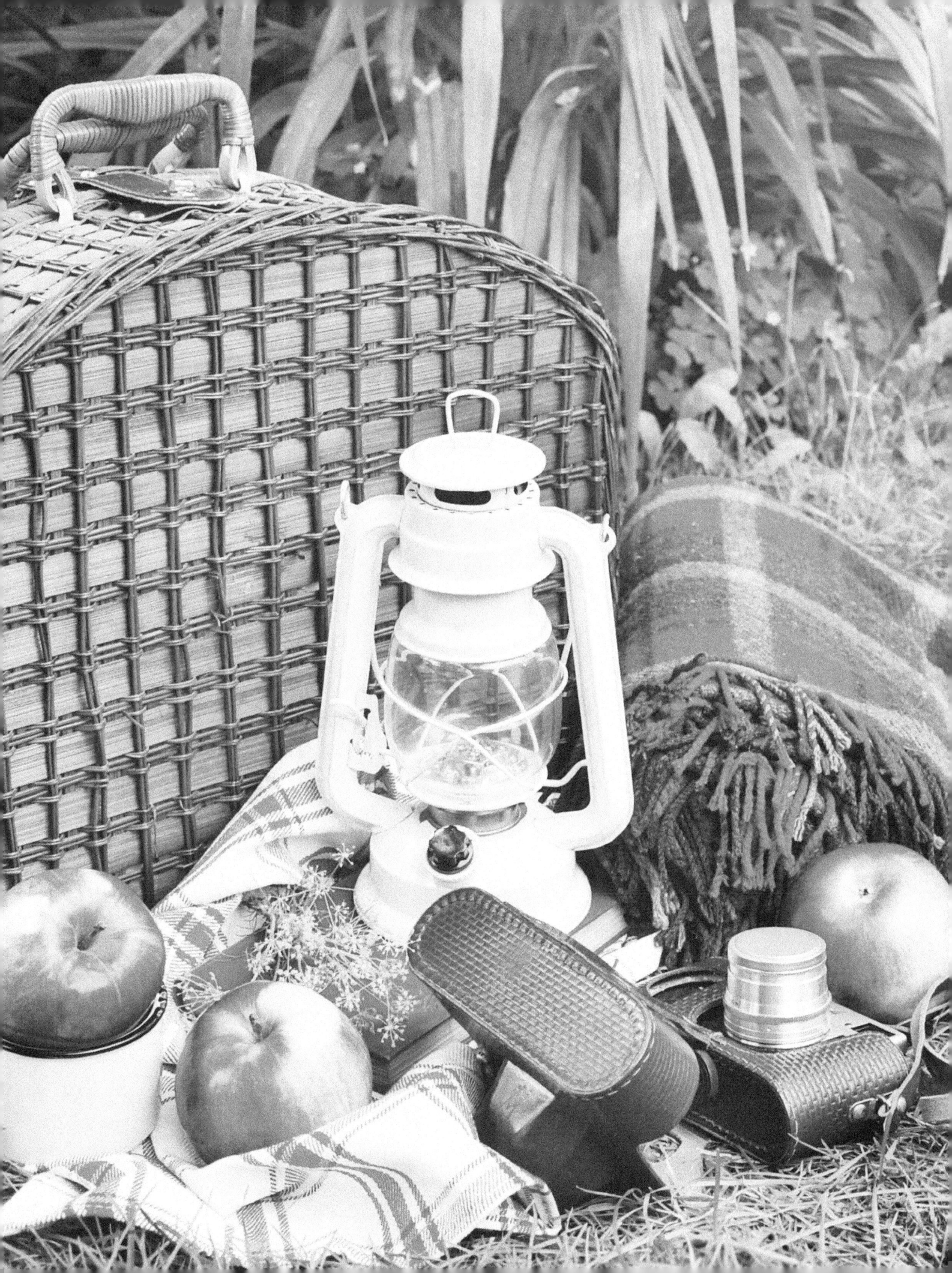

Materials Used:

Colored By:

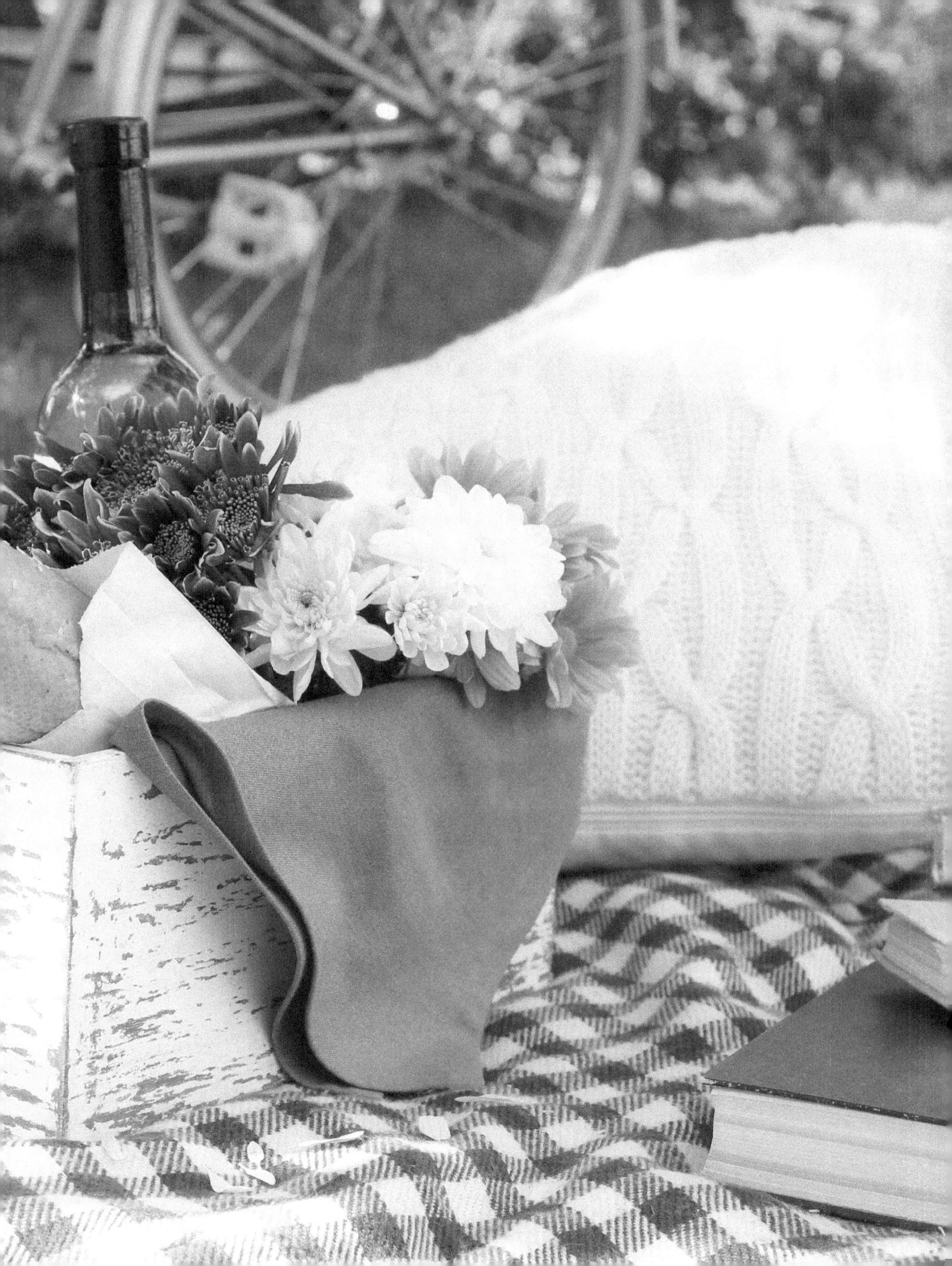

Materials Used:

Colored By:

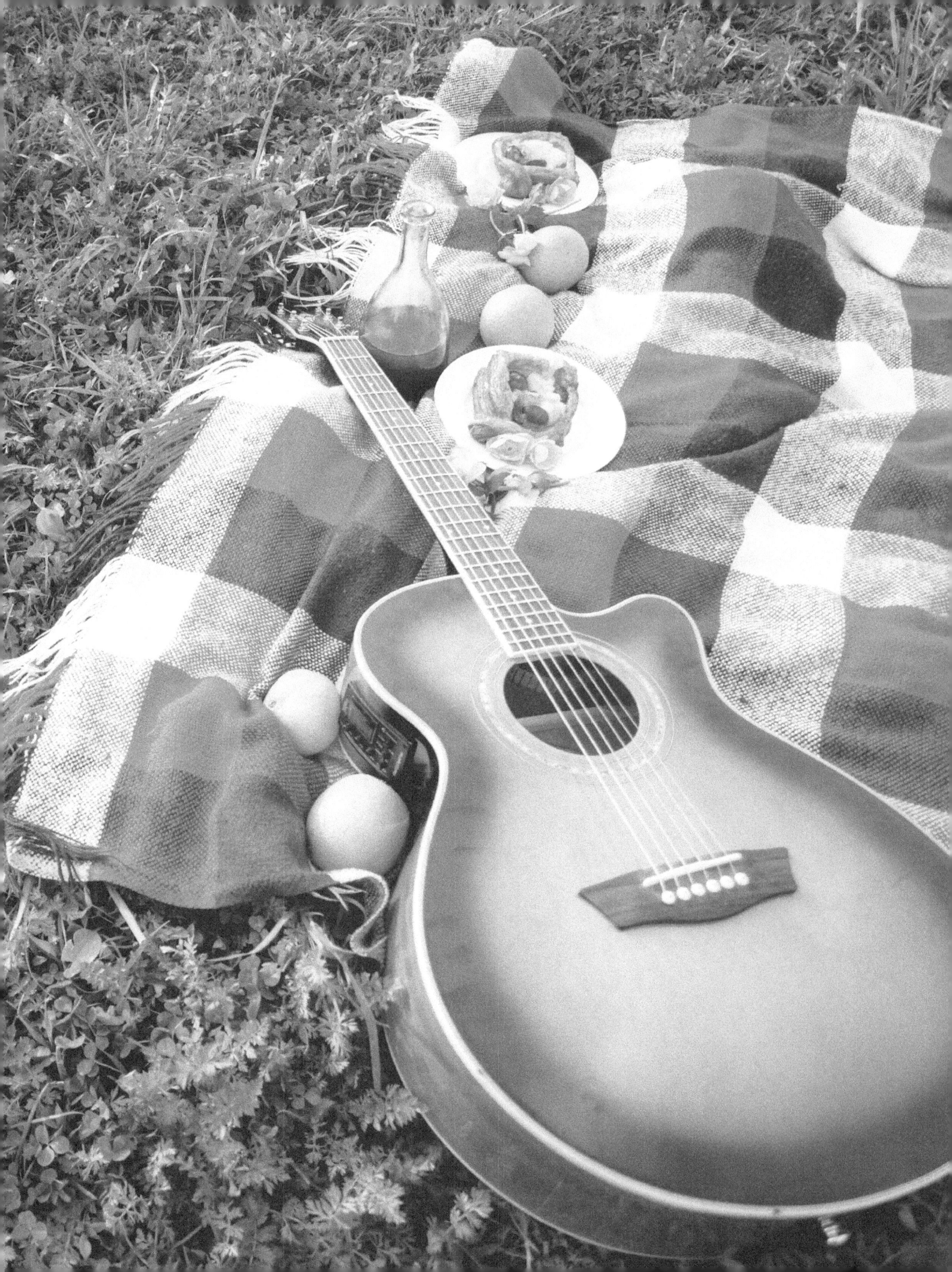

Materials Used:

Colored By:

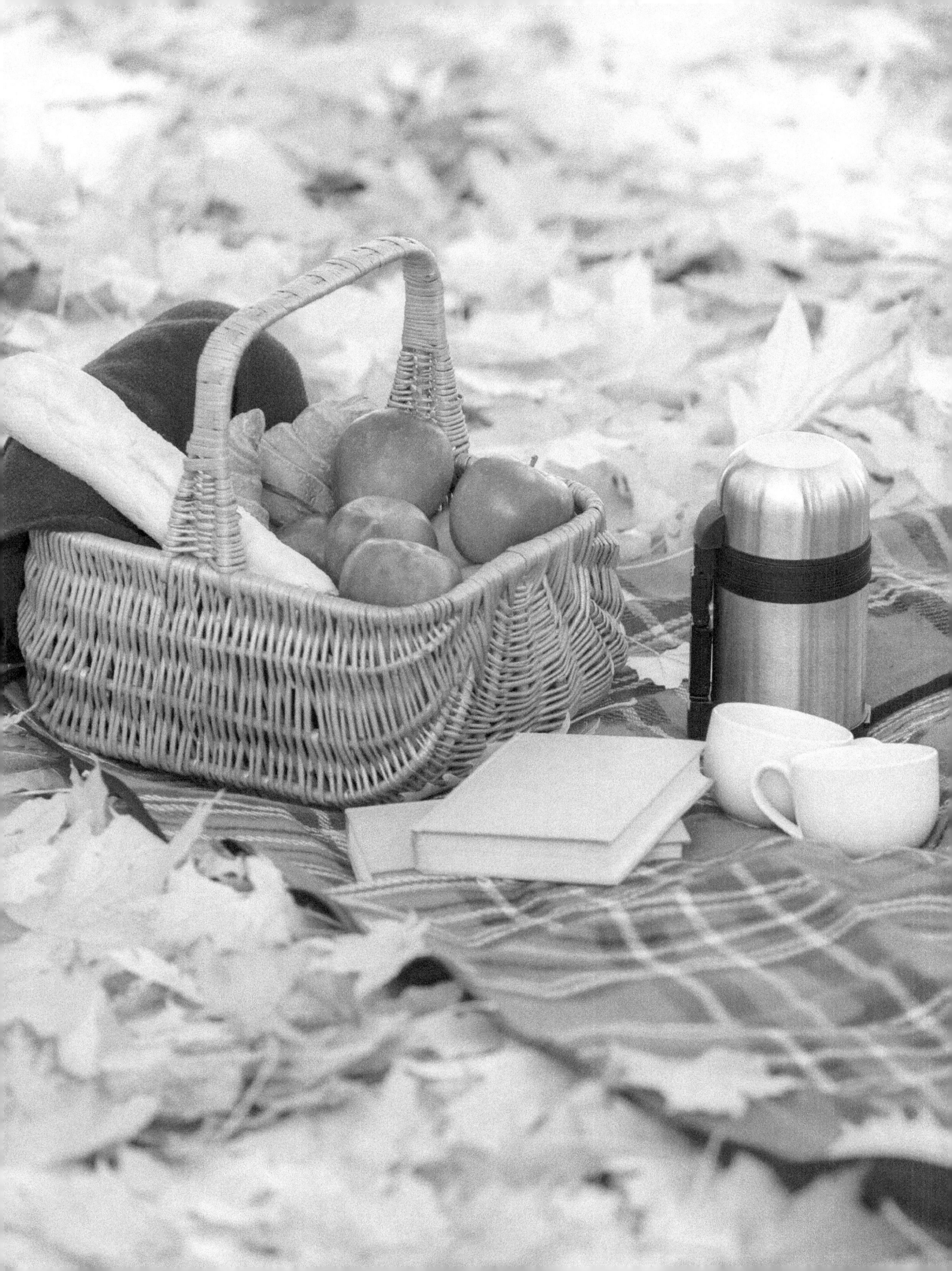

Materials Used:

Colored By:

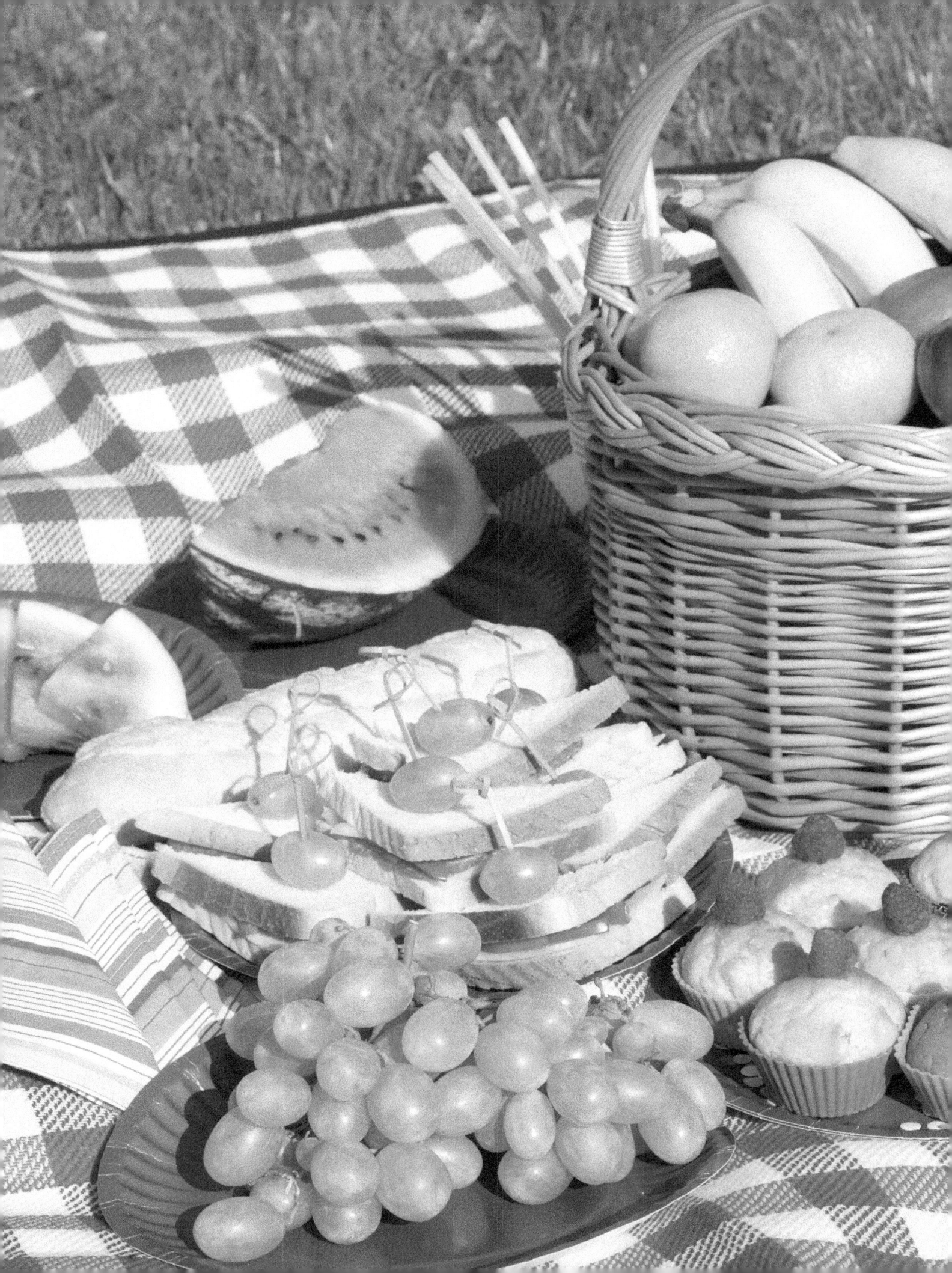

Materials Used:

Colored By:

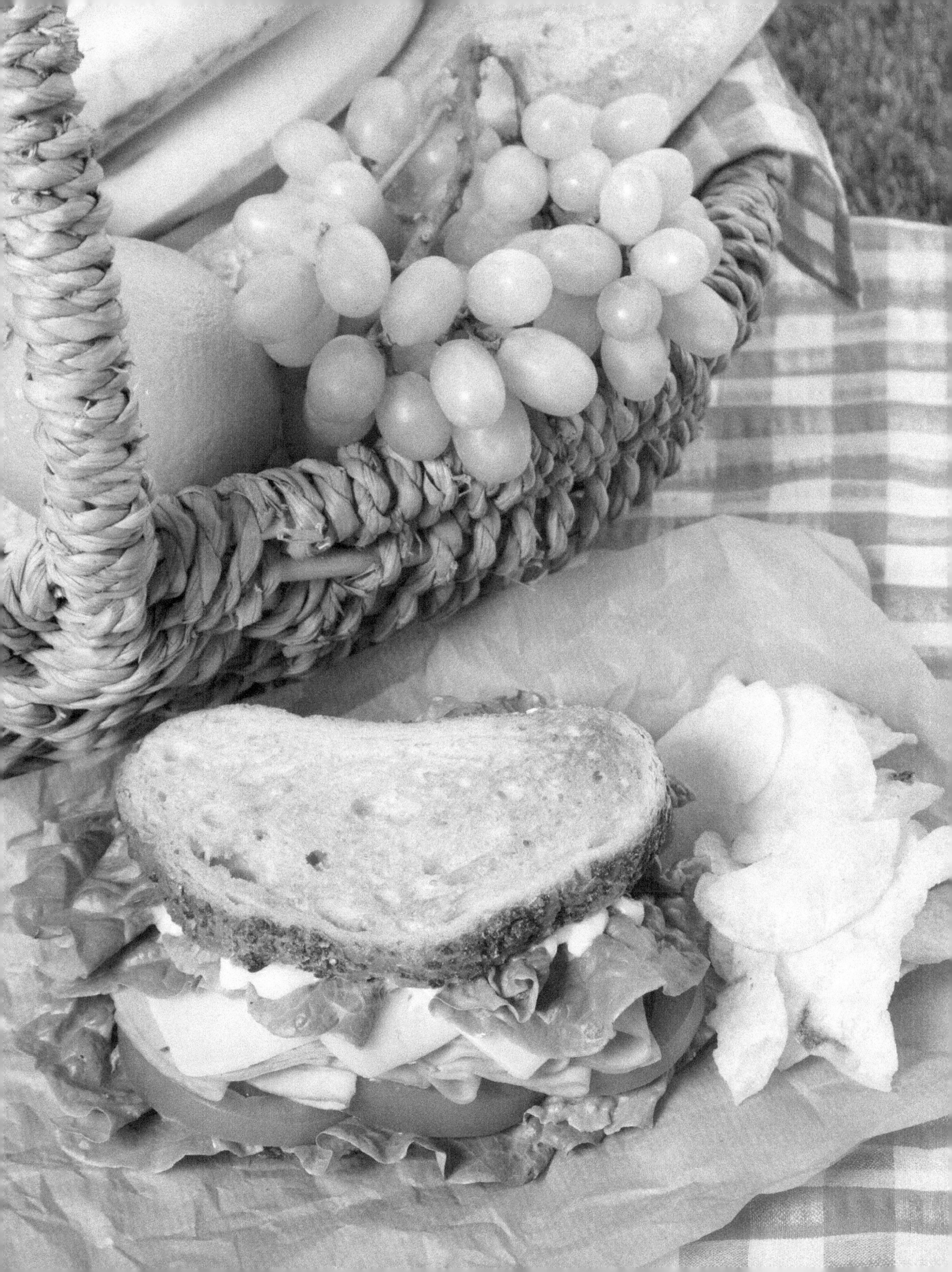

Materials Used:

Colored By:

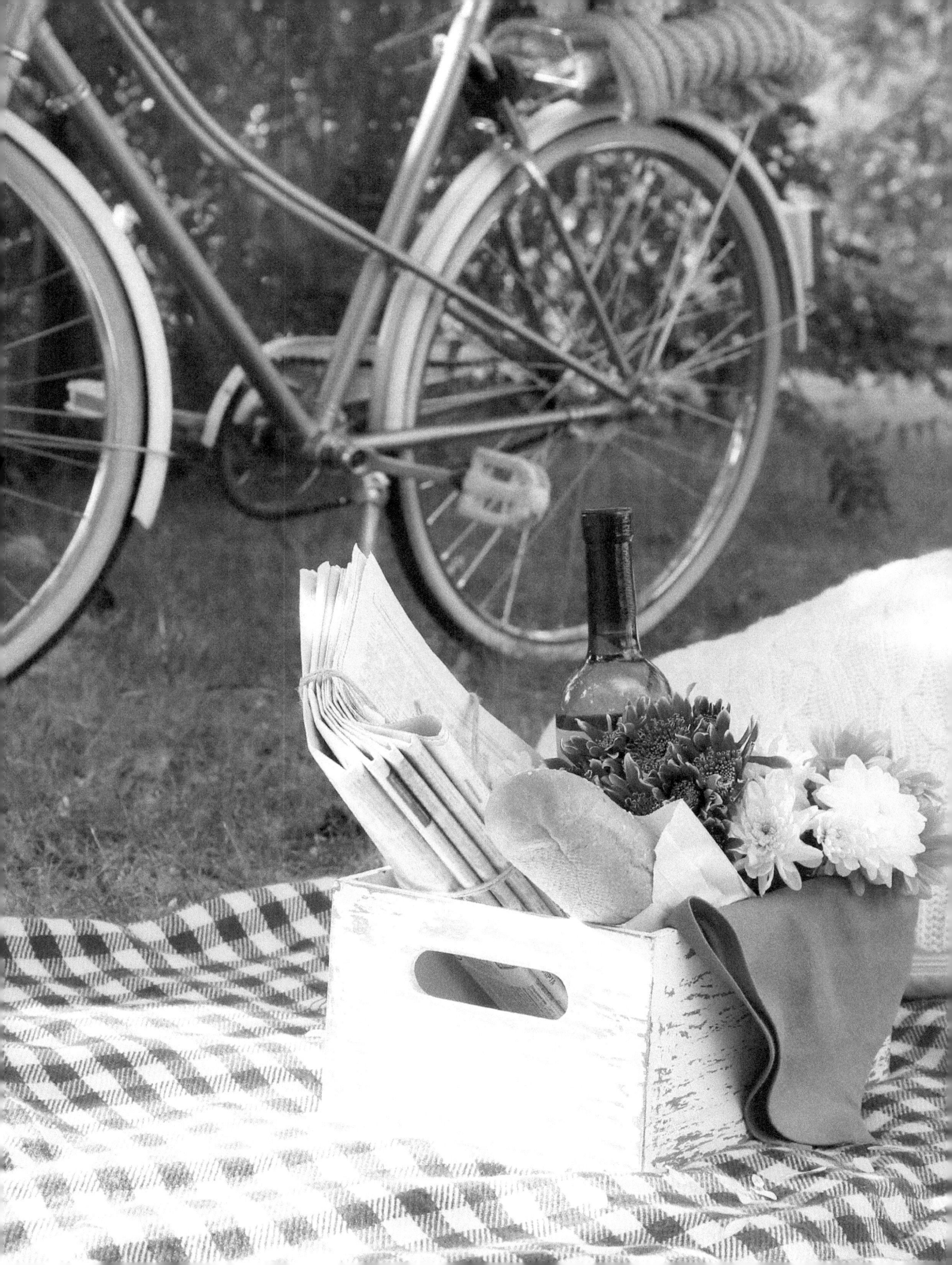

Materials Used:

Colored By:

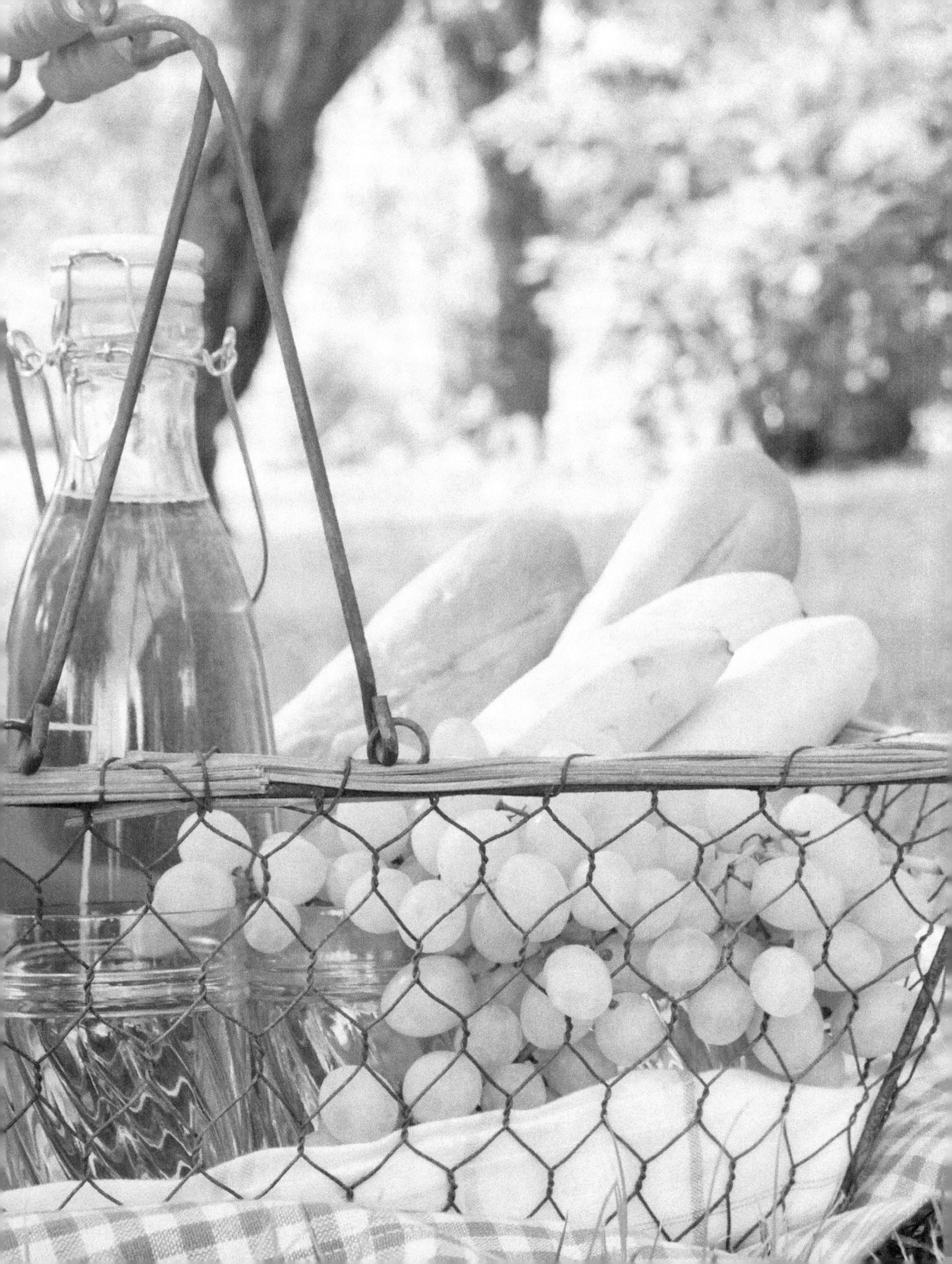

Materials Used:

Colored By:

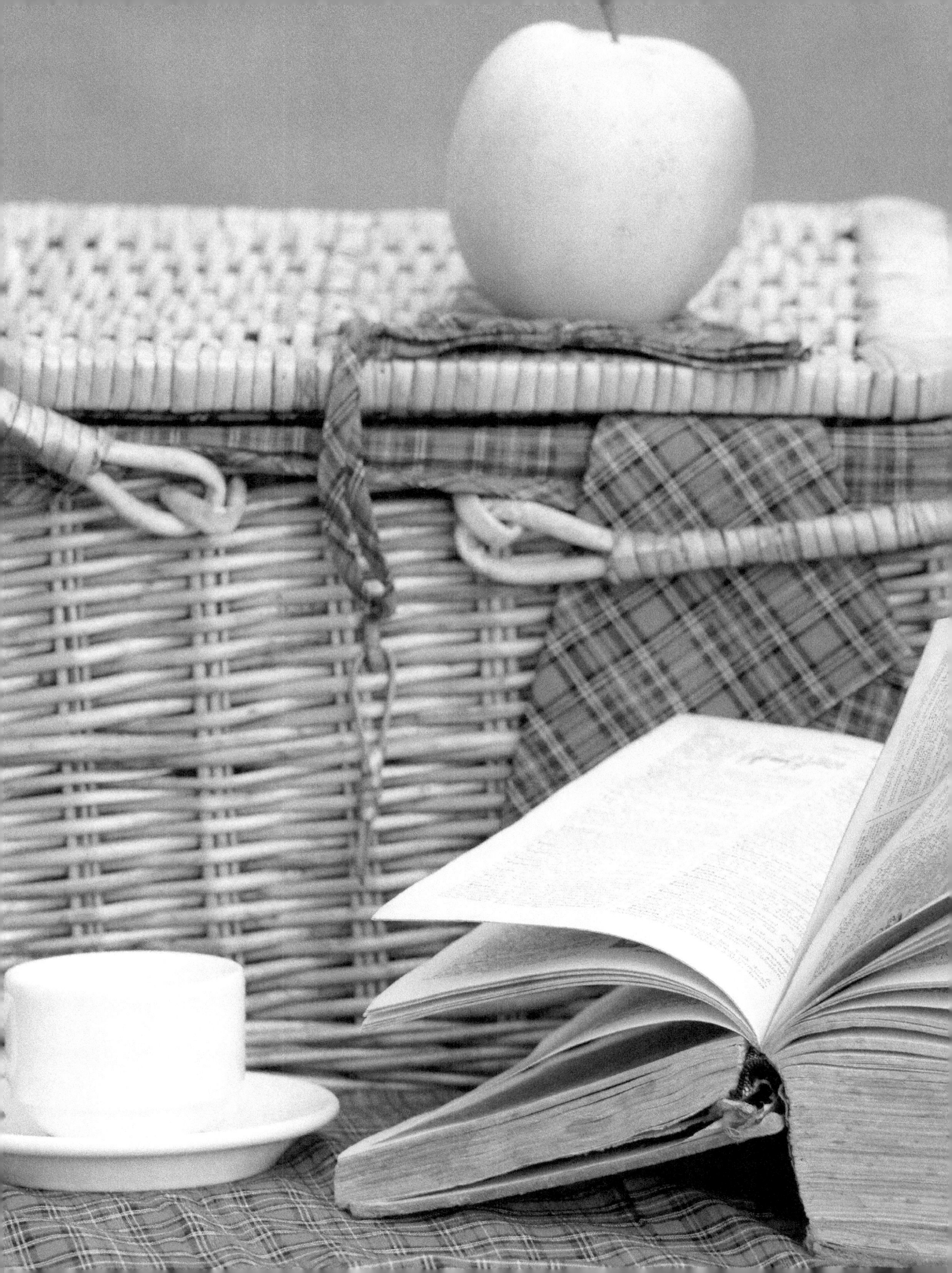

Materials Used:

Colored By:

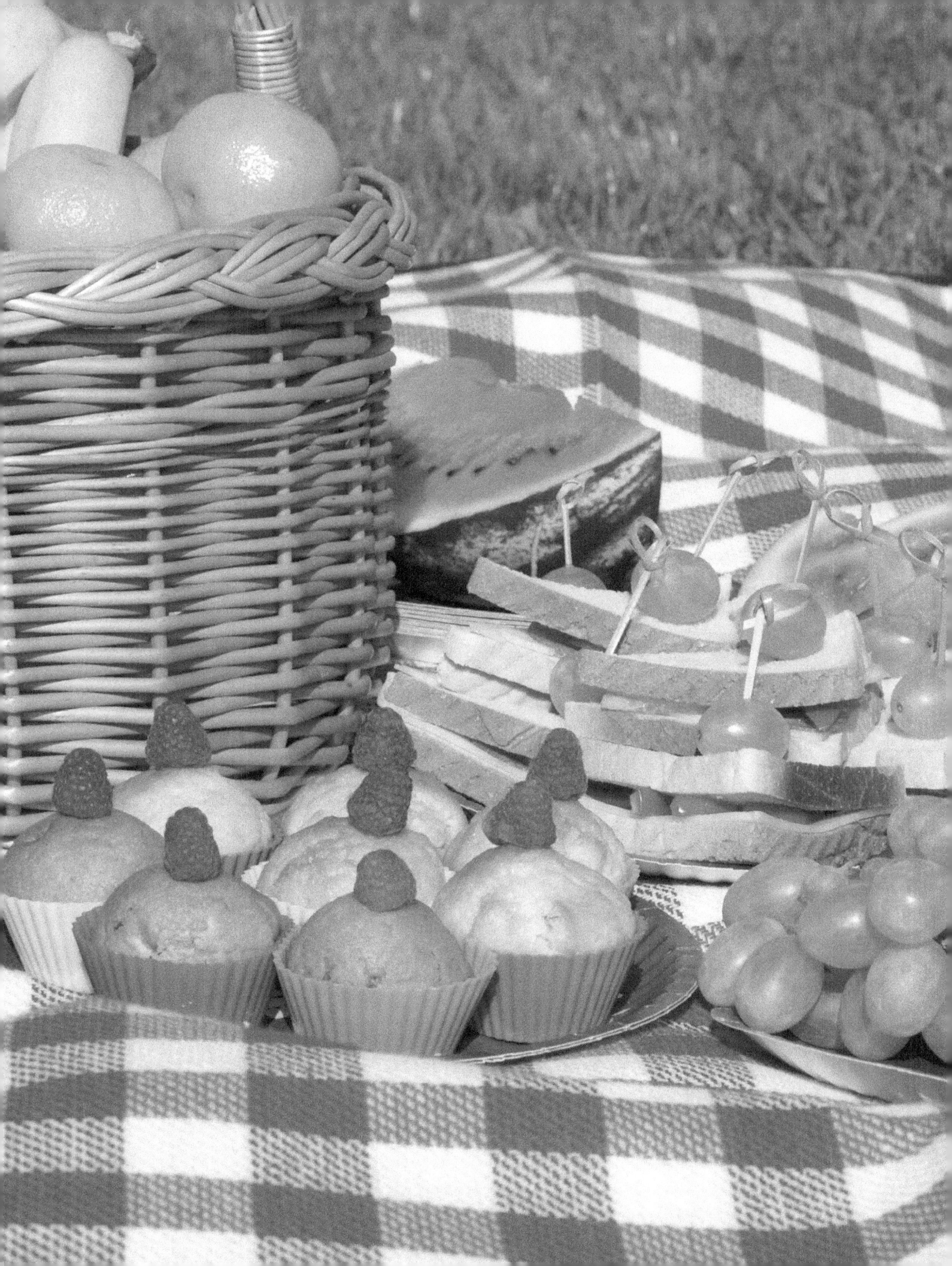

Materials Used:

Colored By:

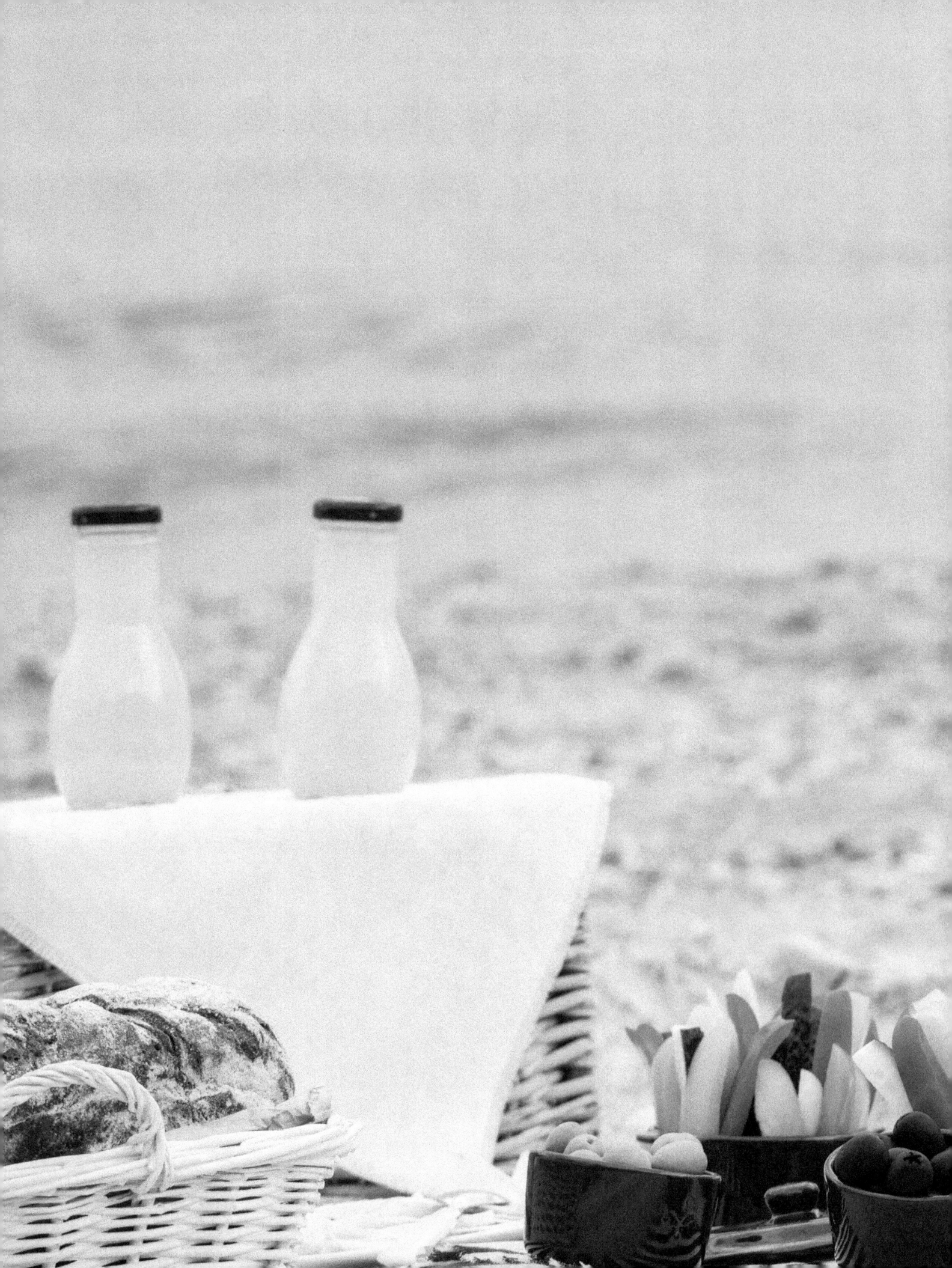

Materials Used:

Colored By:

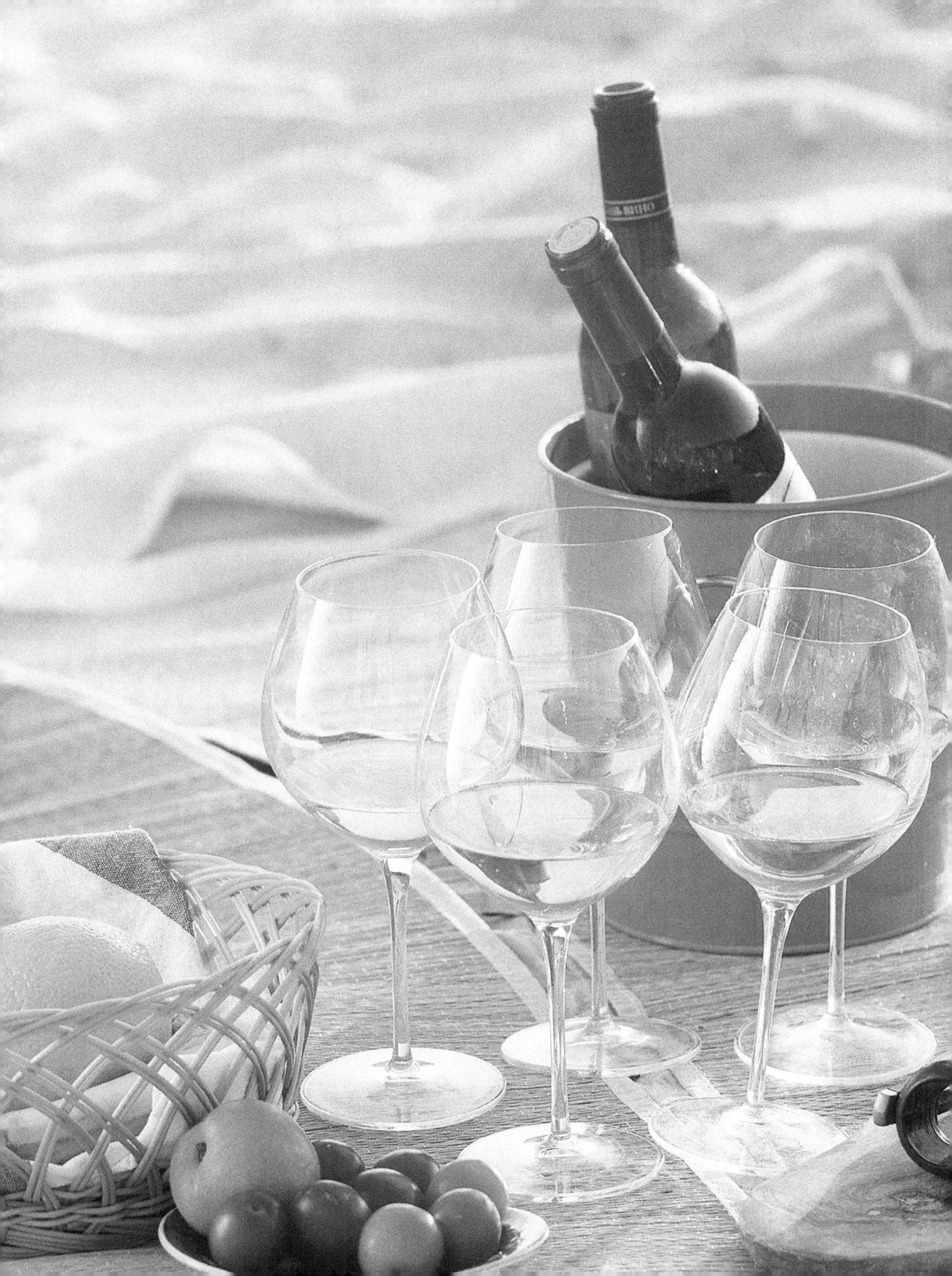

Materials Used:

Colored By:

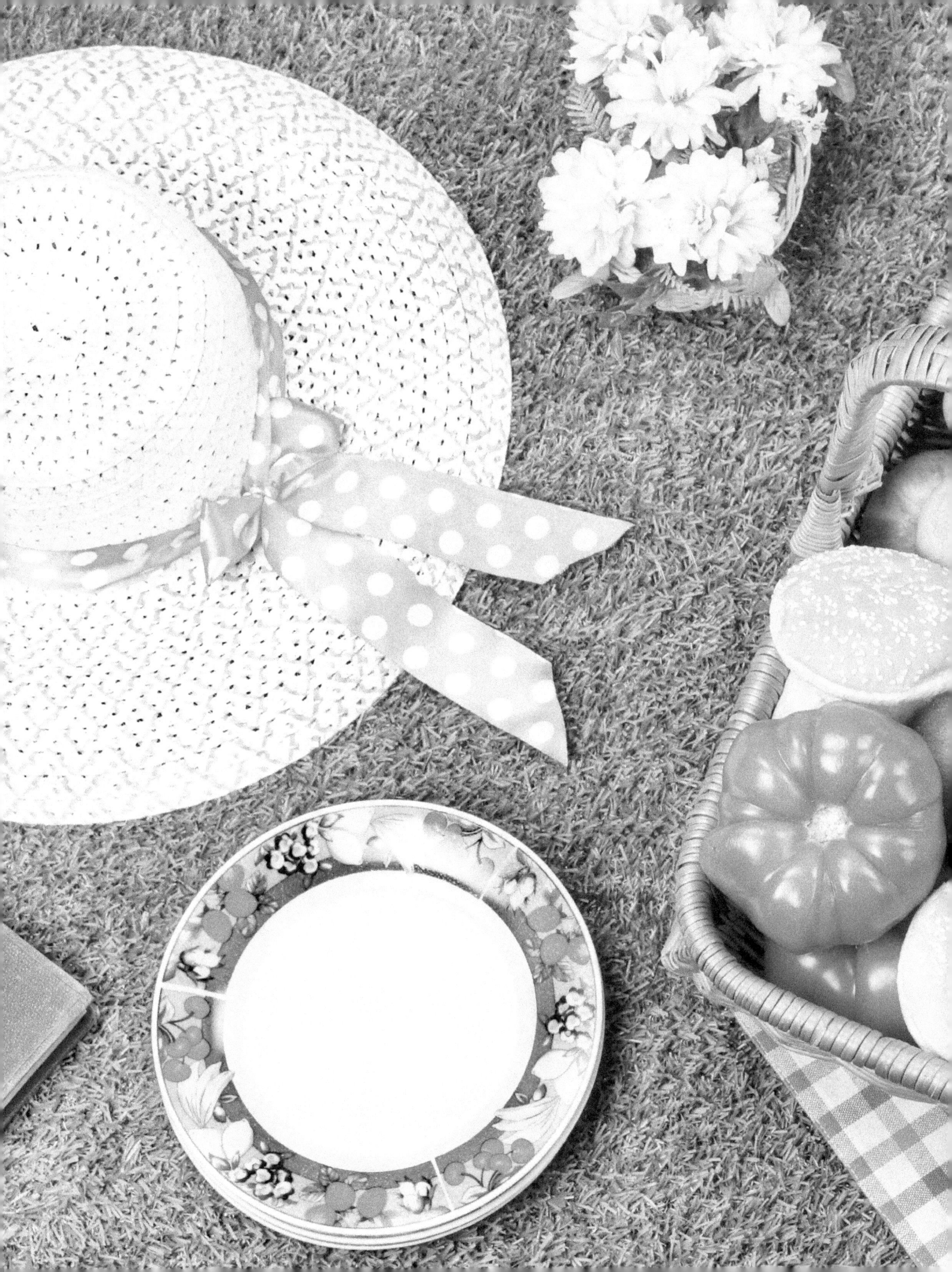

Materials Used:

Colored By:

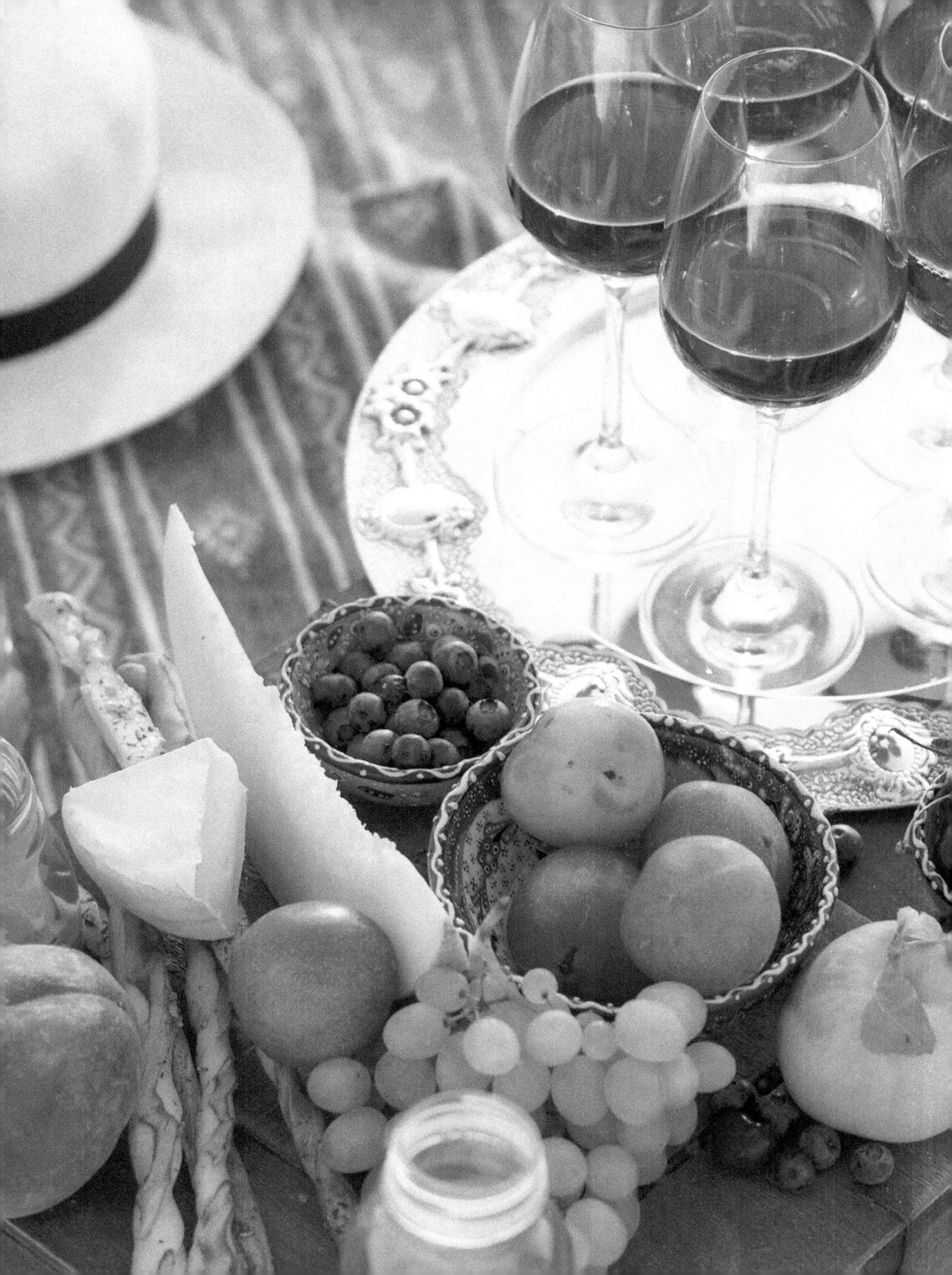

Materials Used:

Colored By:

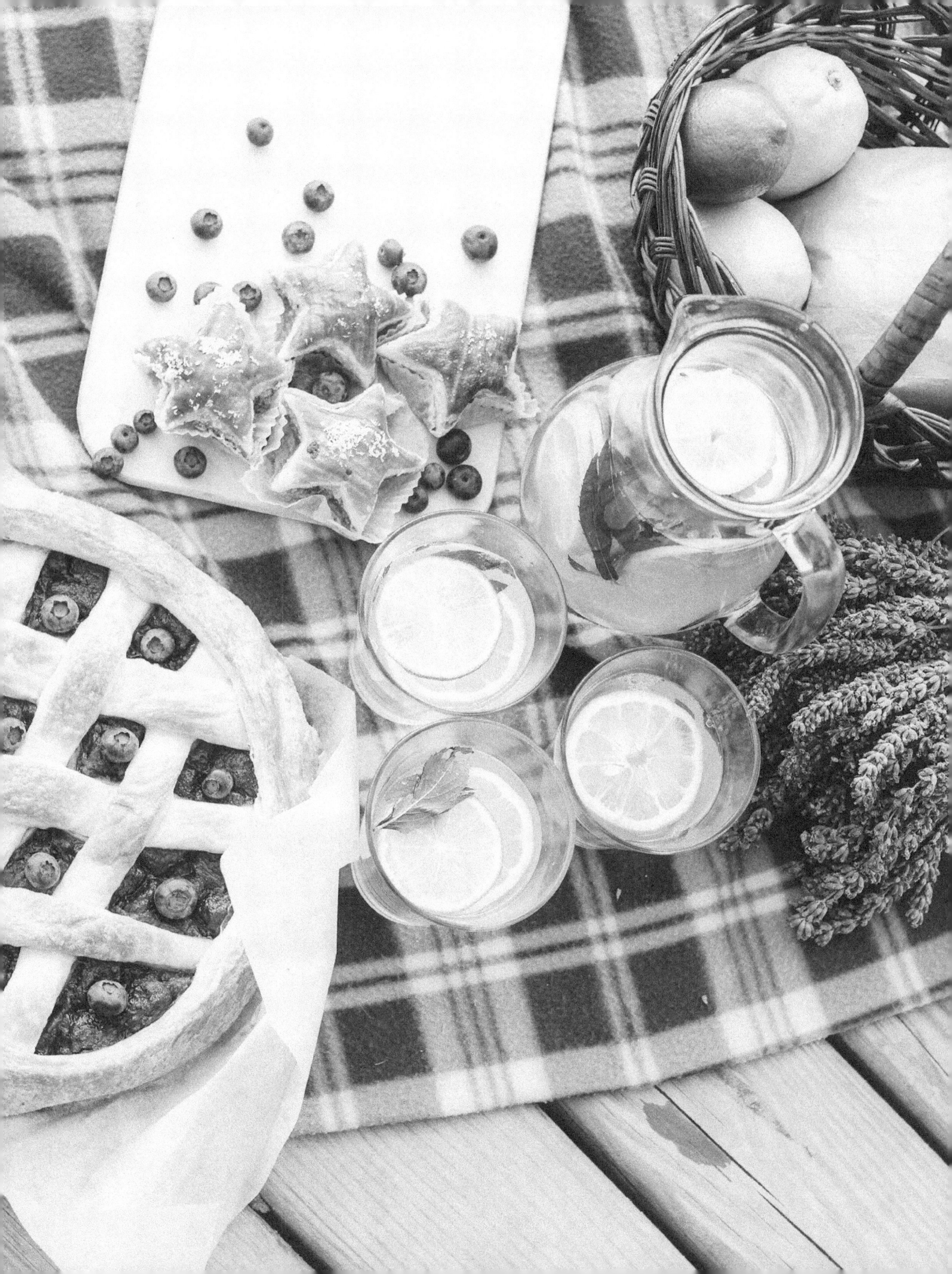

Materials Used:

Colored By:

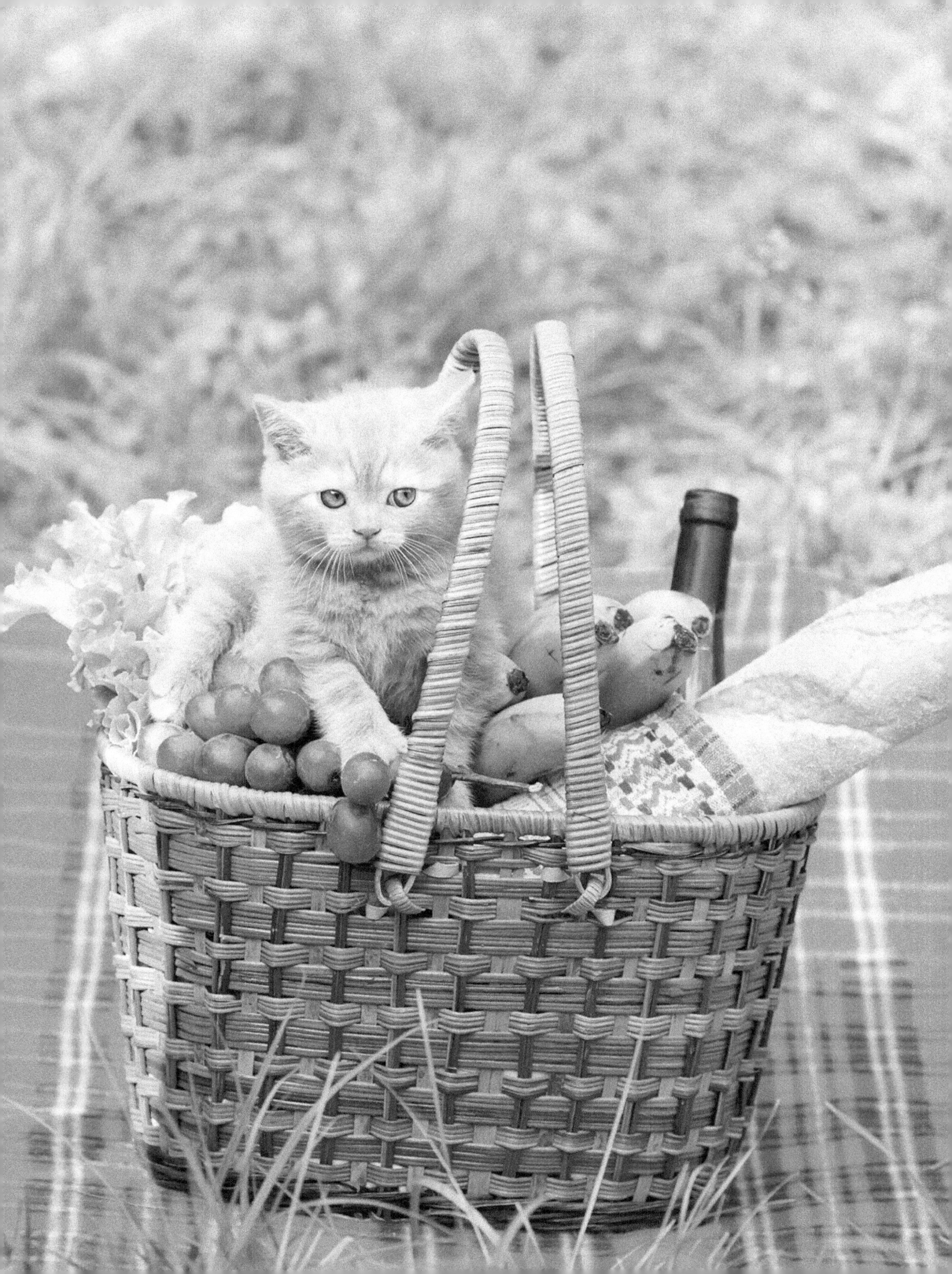

Materials Used:

Colored By:

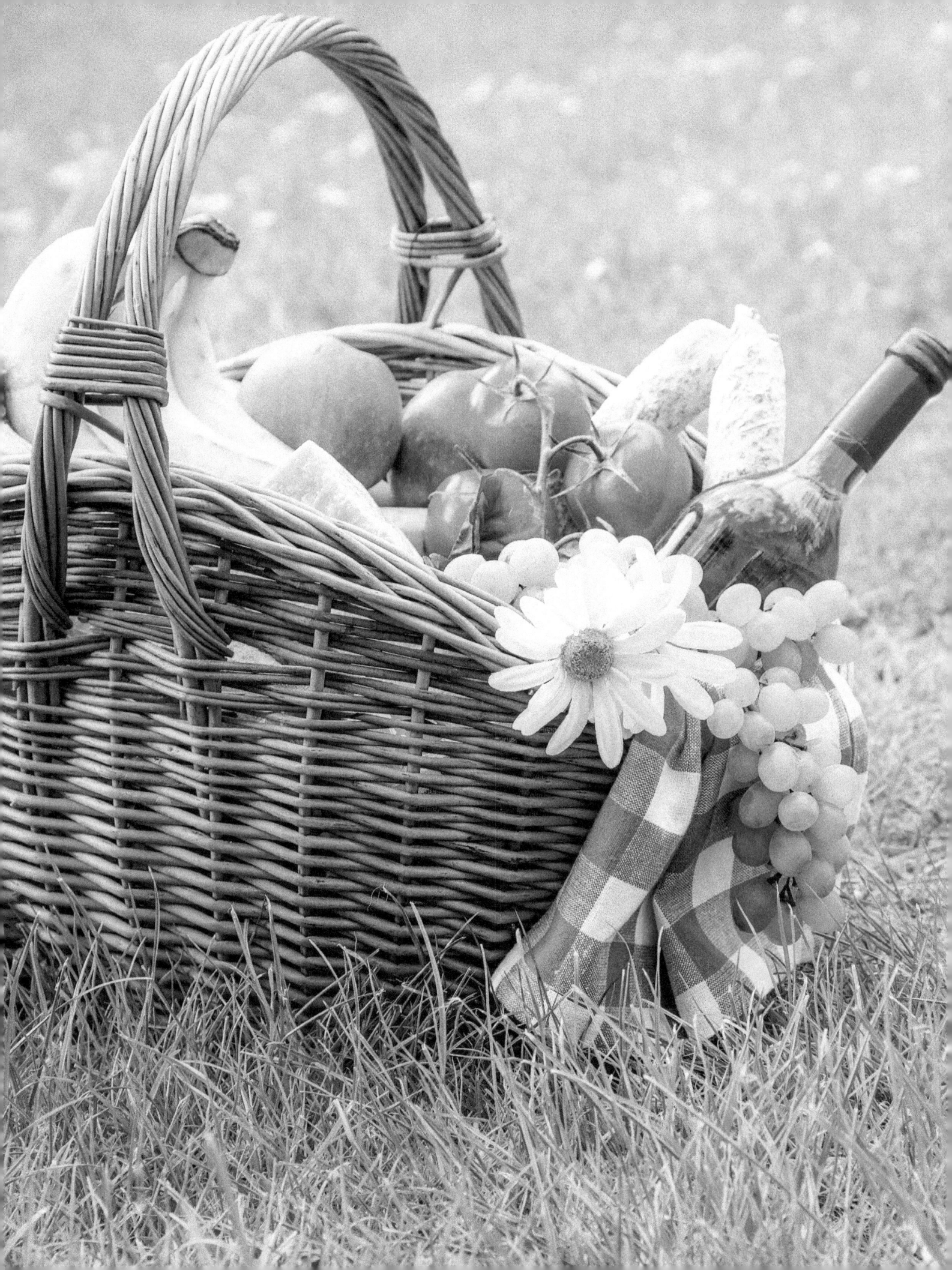

Materials Used:

Colored By:

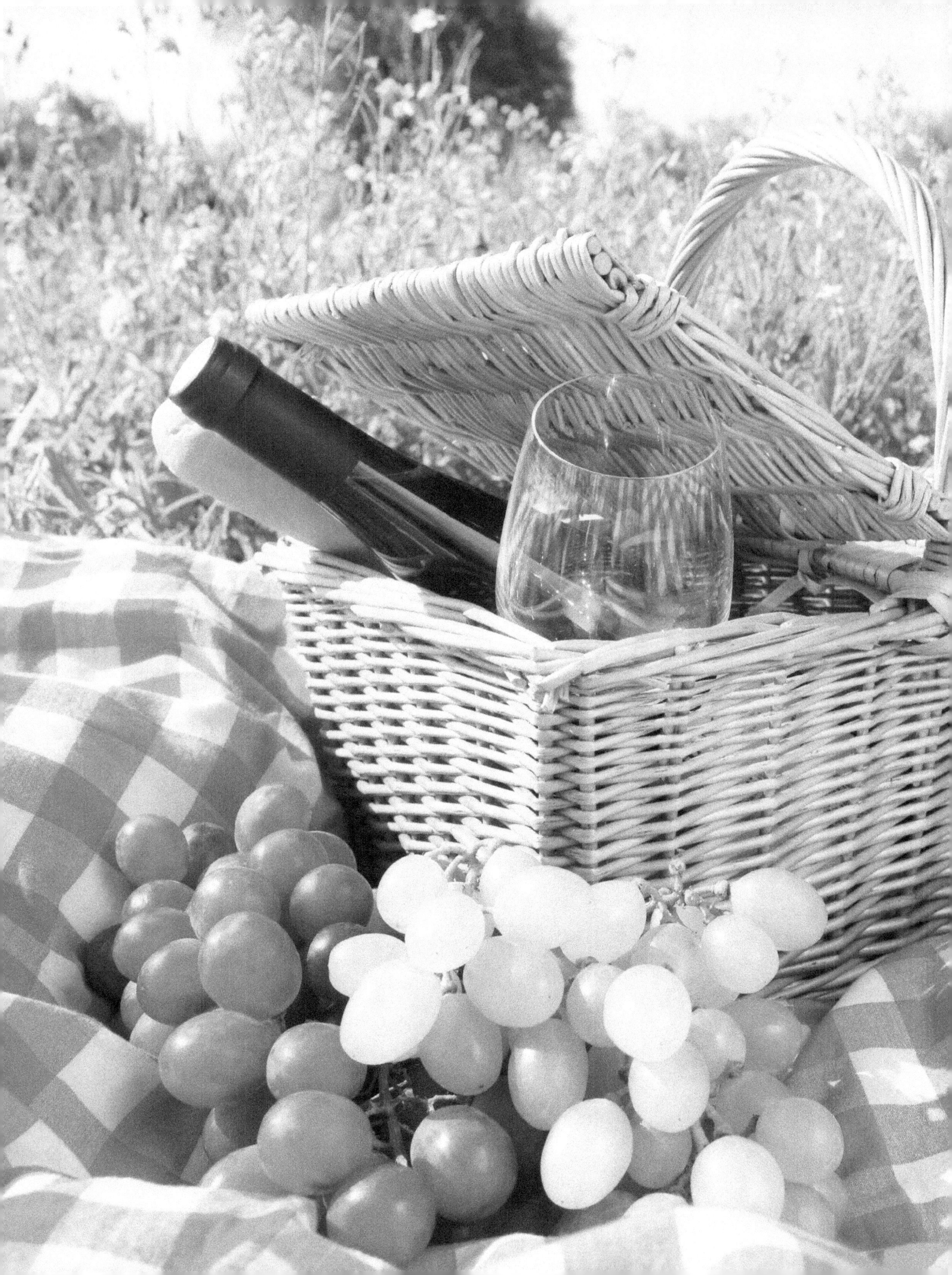

Materials Used:

Colored By:

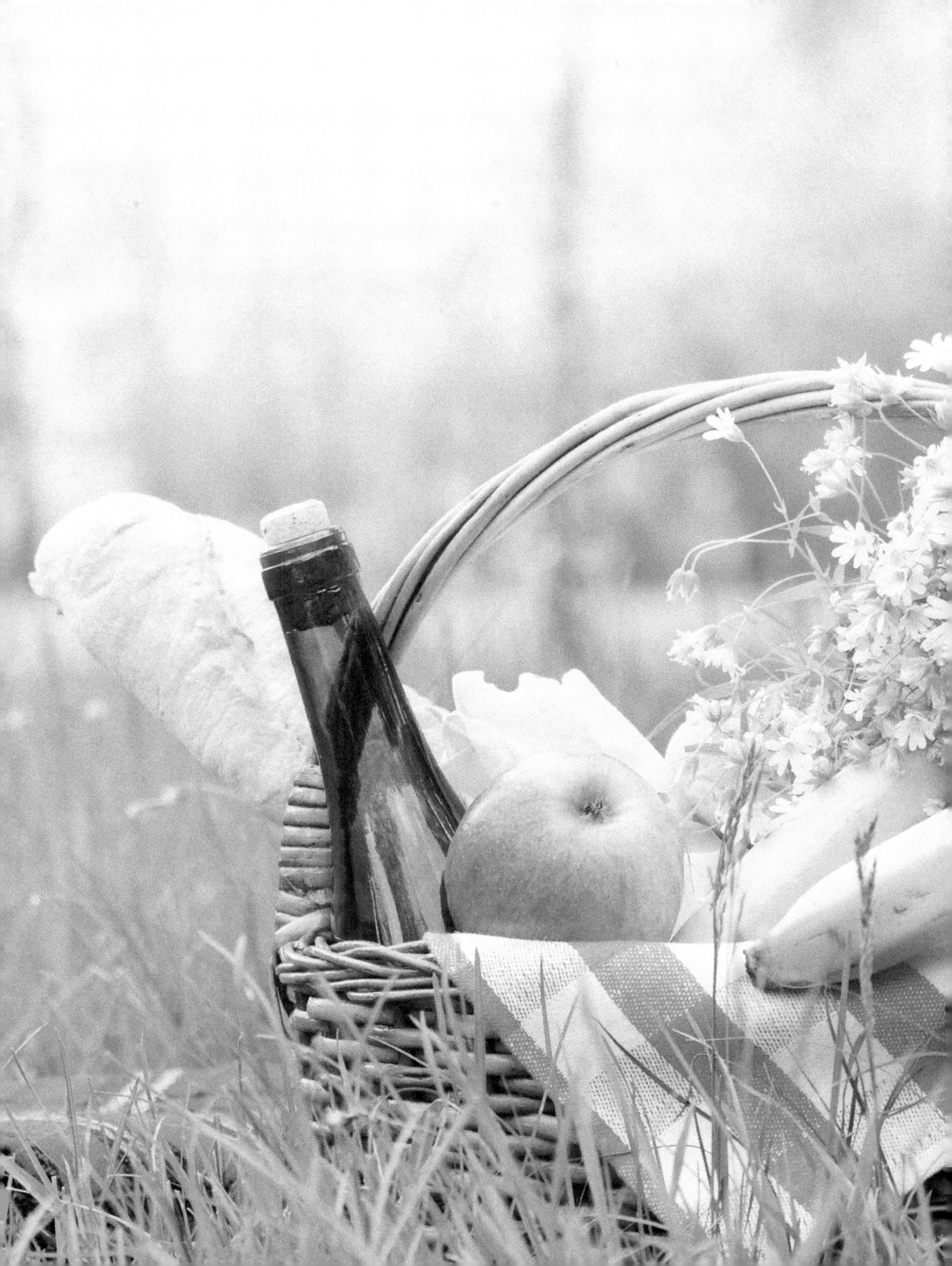

Materials Used:

Colored By:

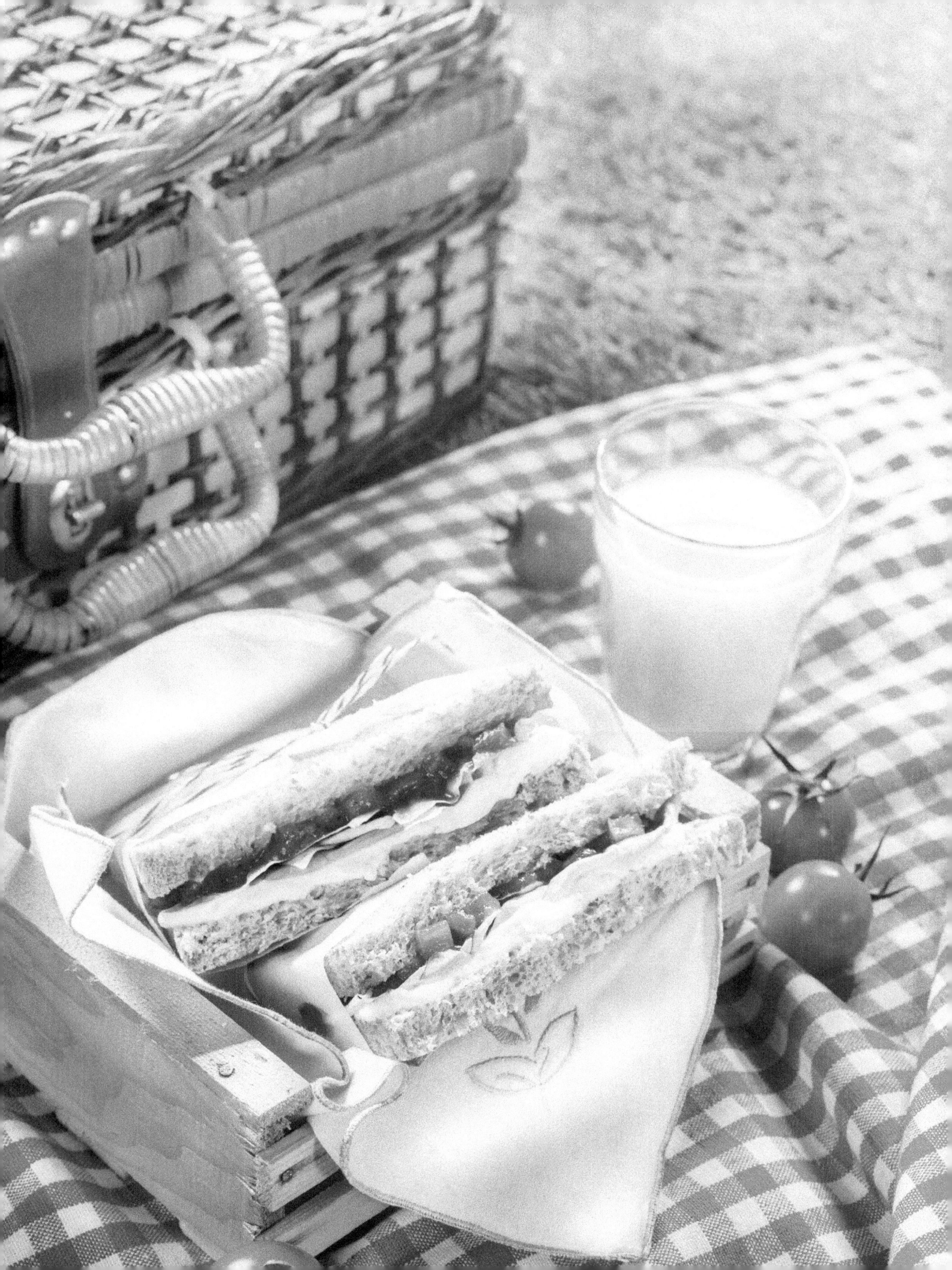

Materials Used:

Colored By:

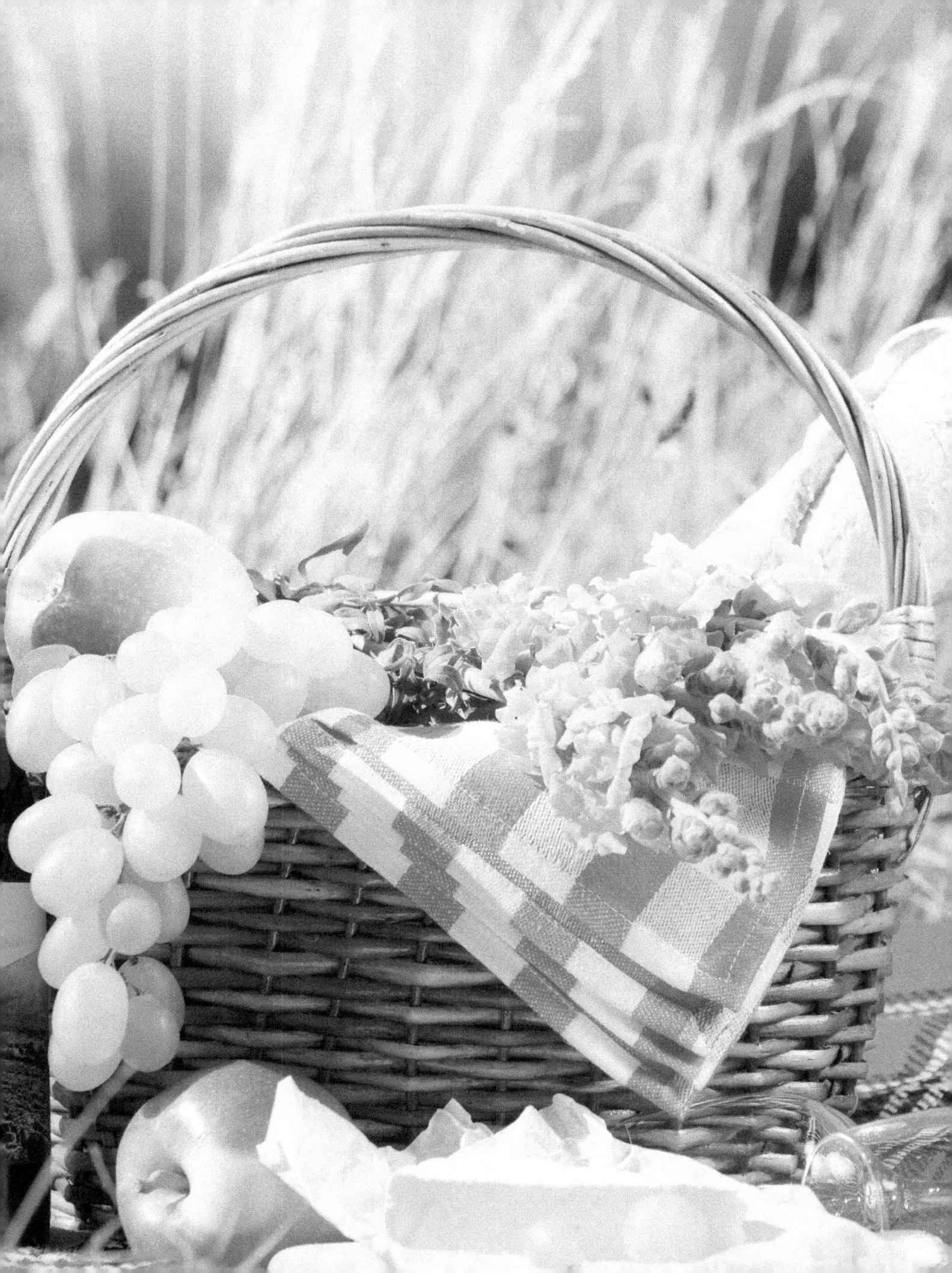

Materials Used:

Colored By:

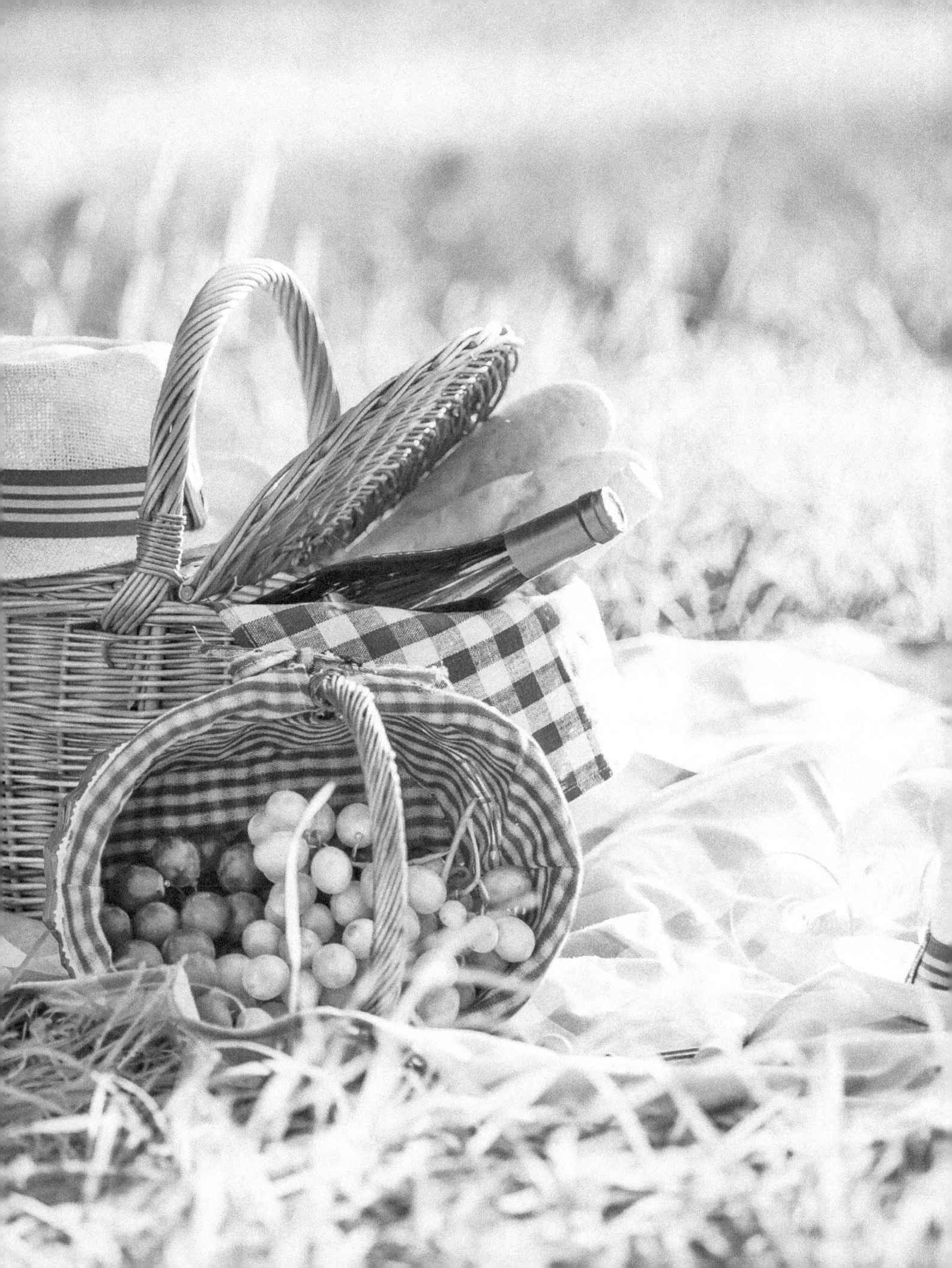

Materials Used:

Colored By:

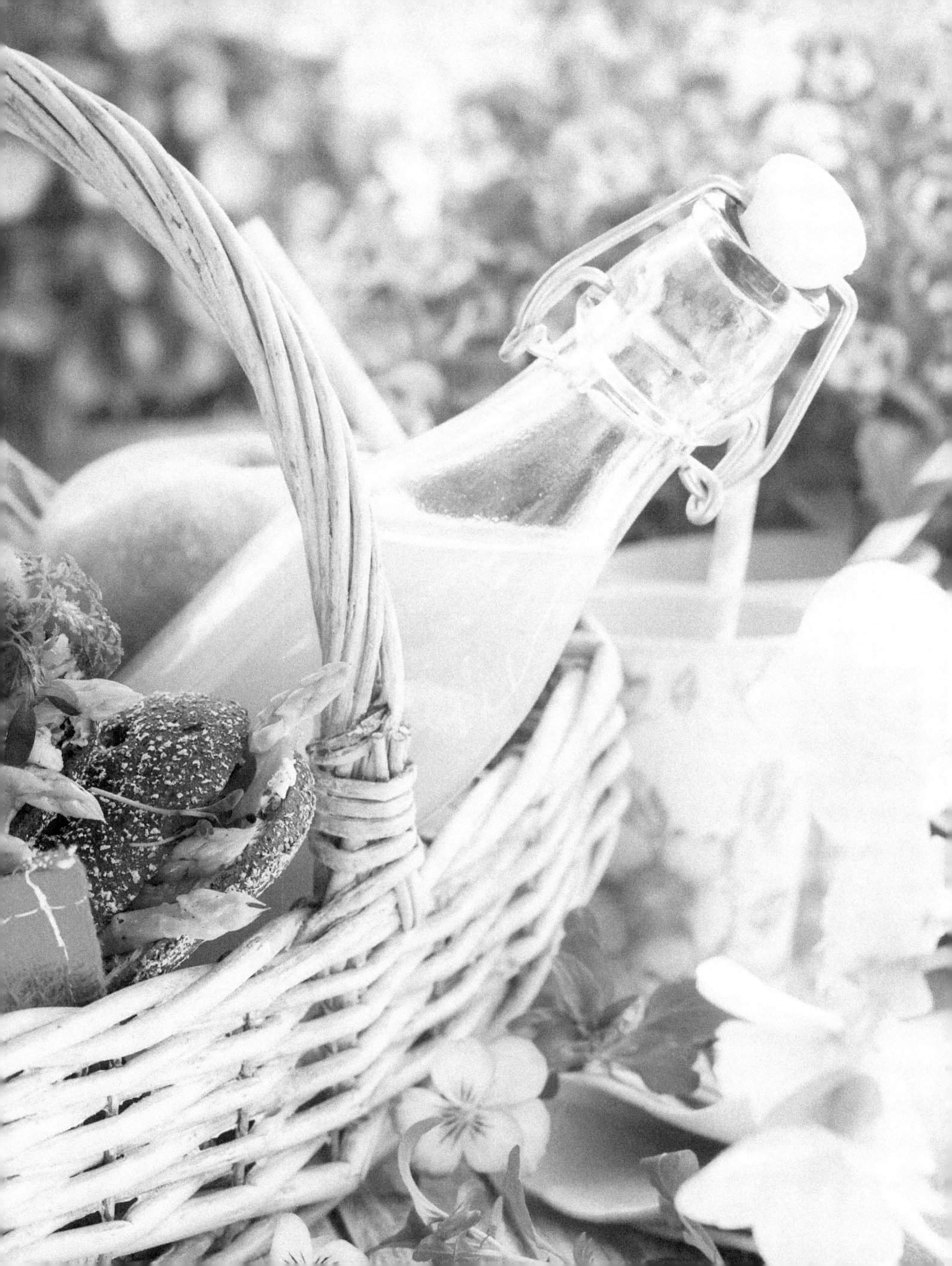

Materials Used:

Colored By:

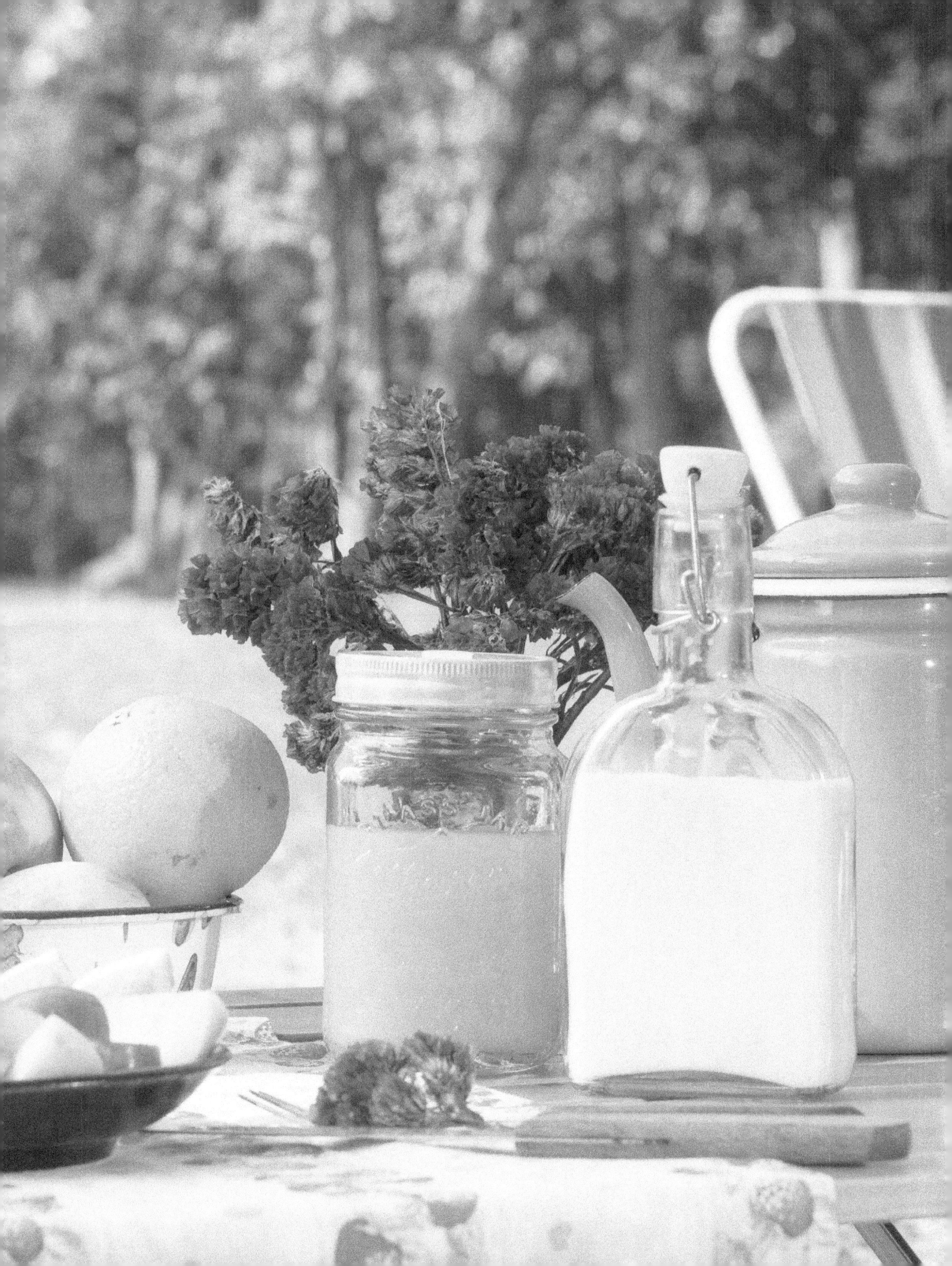

Materials Used:

Colored By:

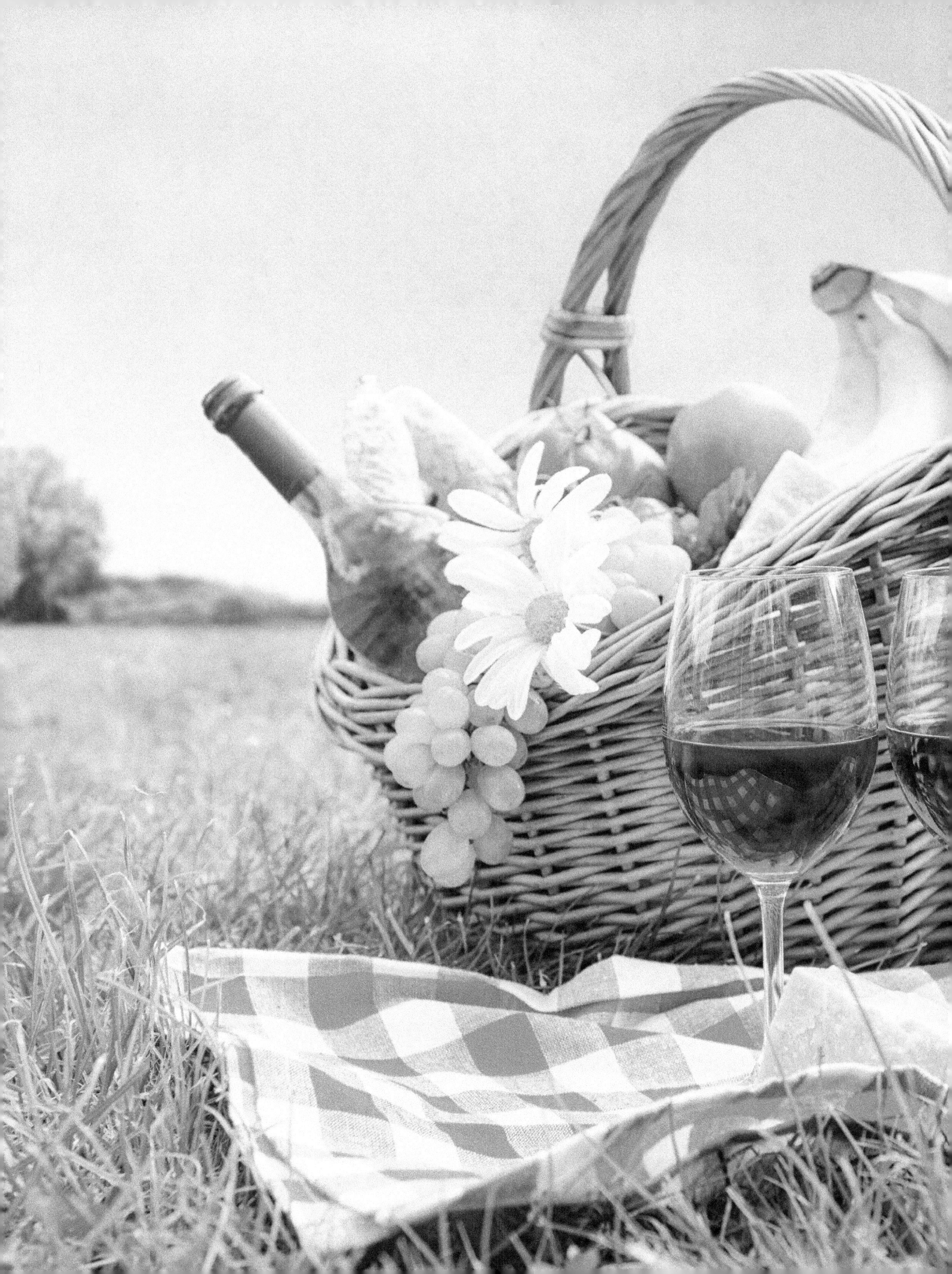

Materials Used:

Colored By:

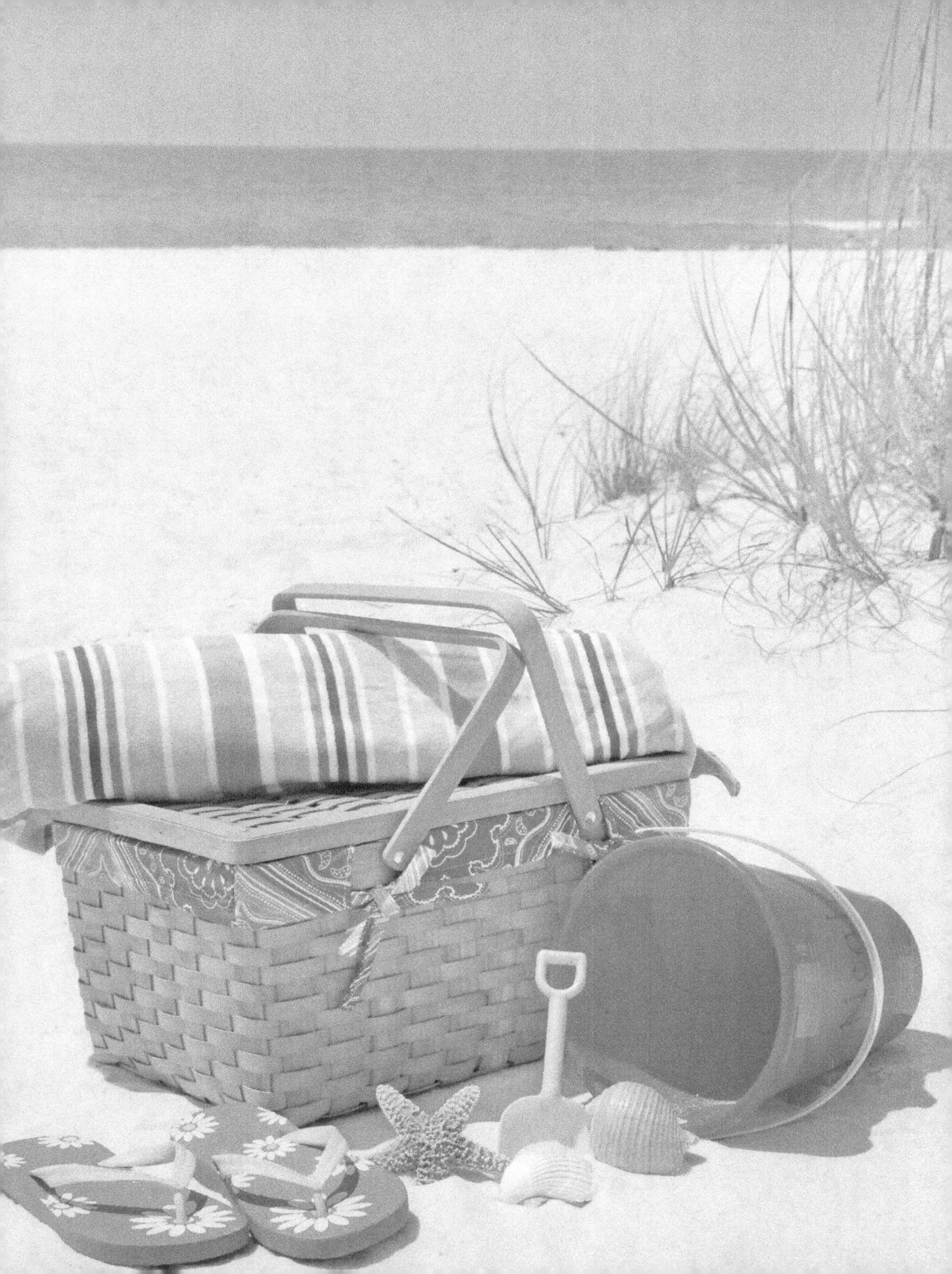

Materials Used:

Colored By:

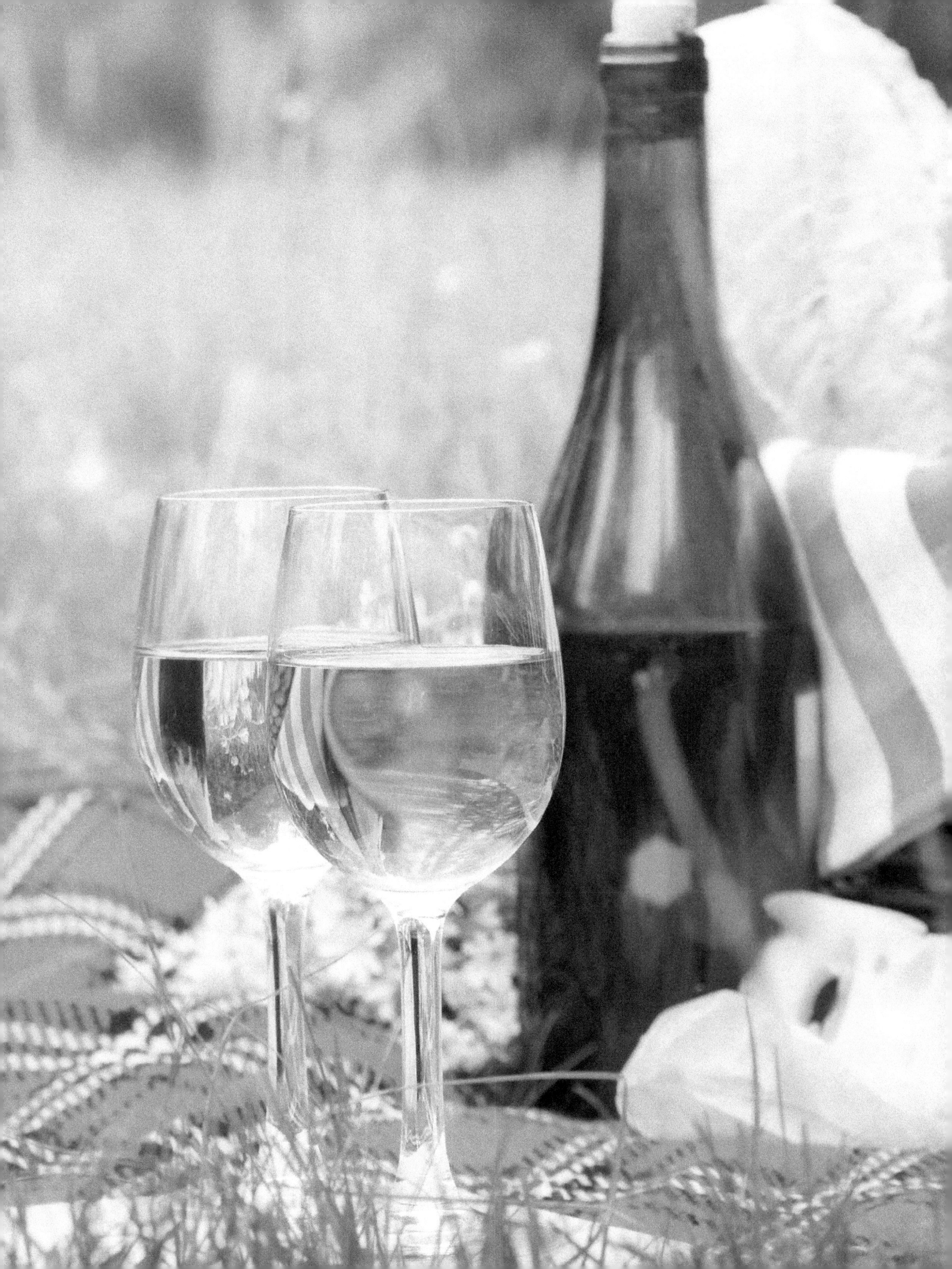

Materials Used:

Colored By:

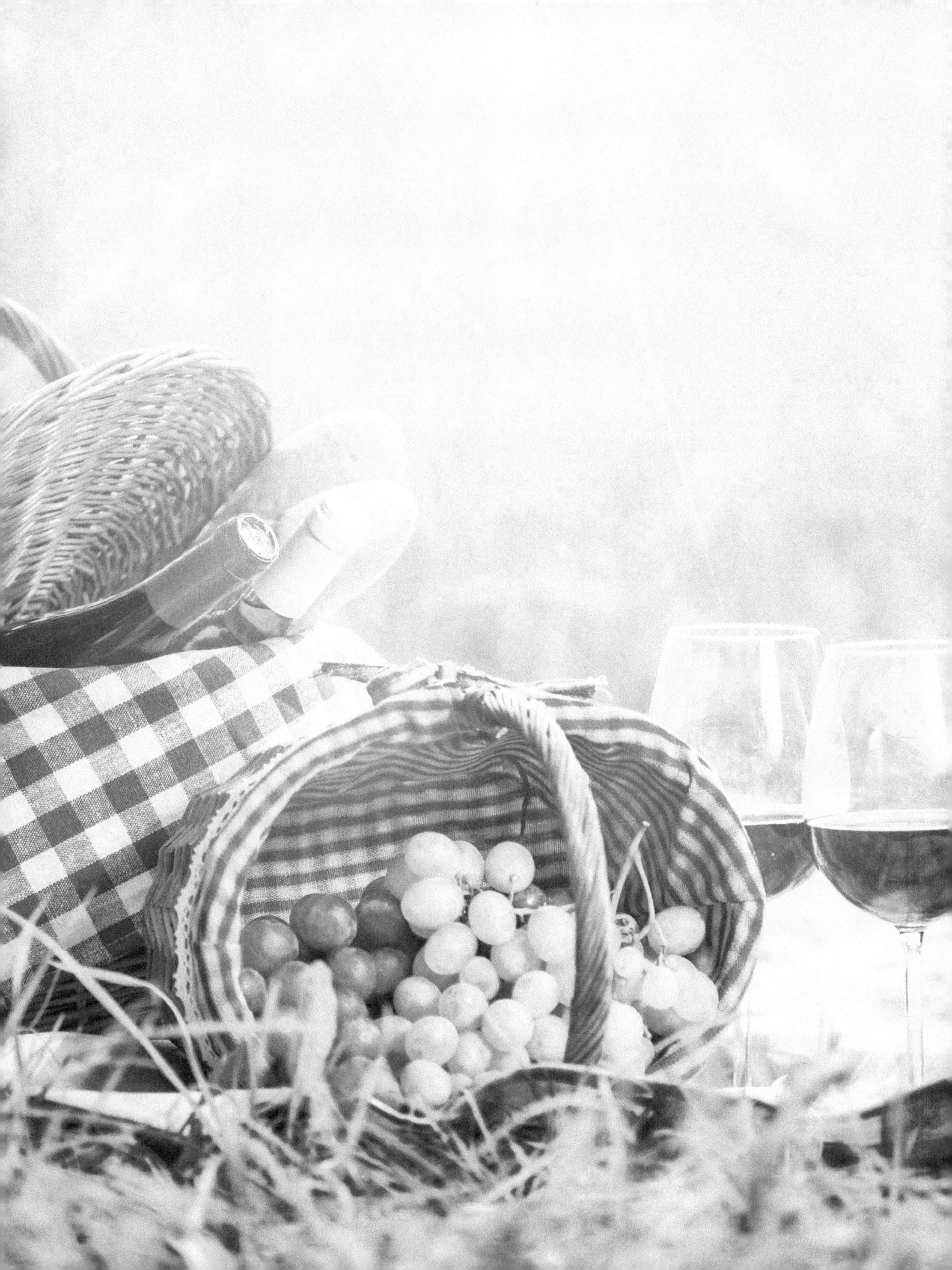

Materials Used:

Colored By:

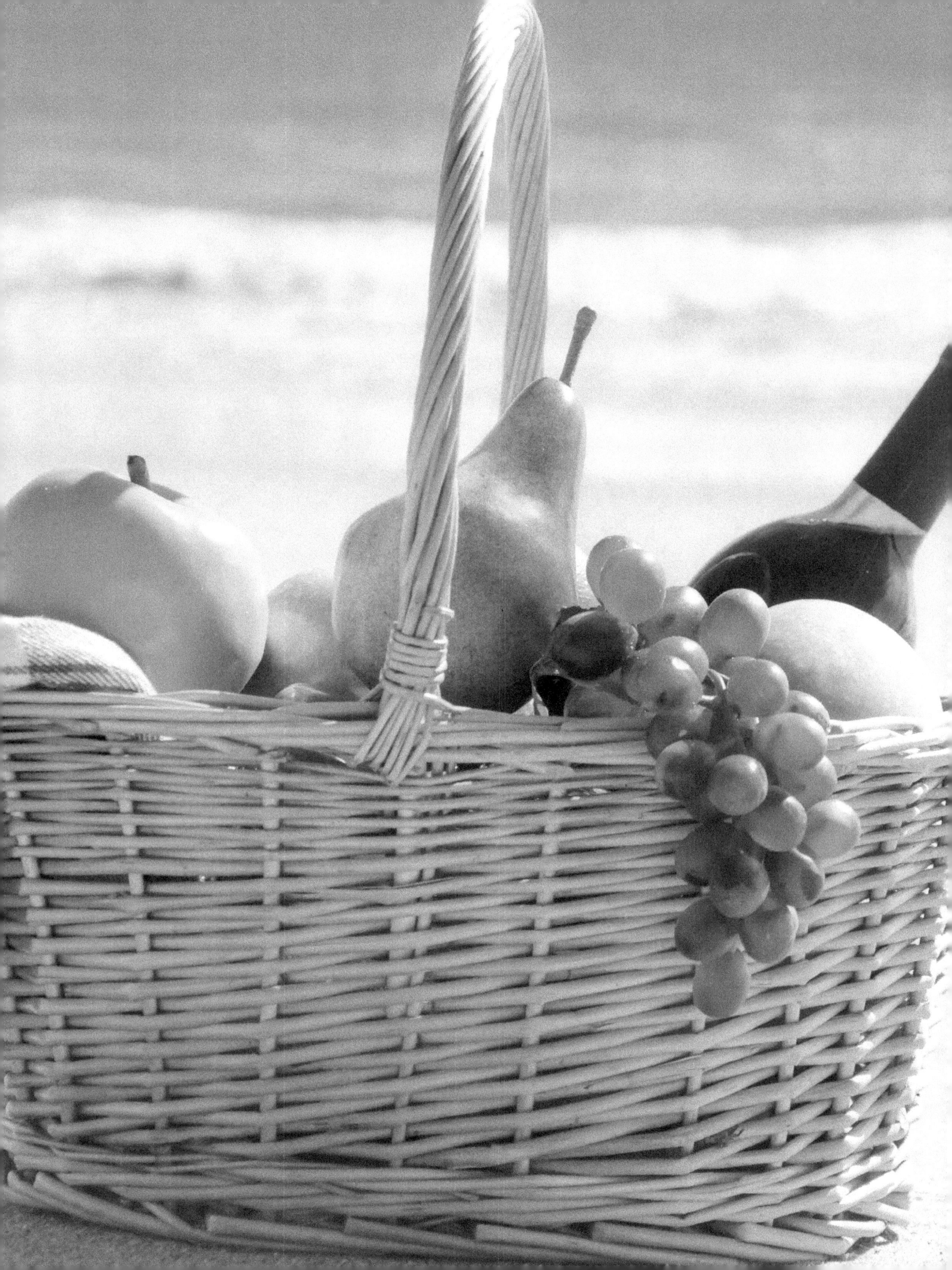

Materials Used:

Colored By:

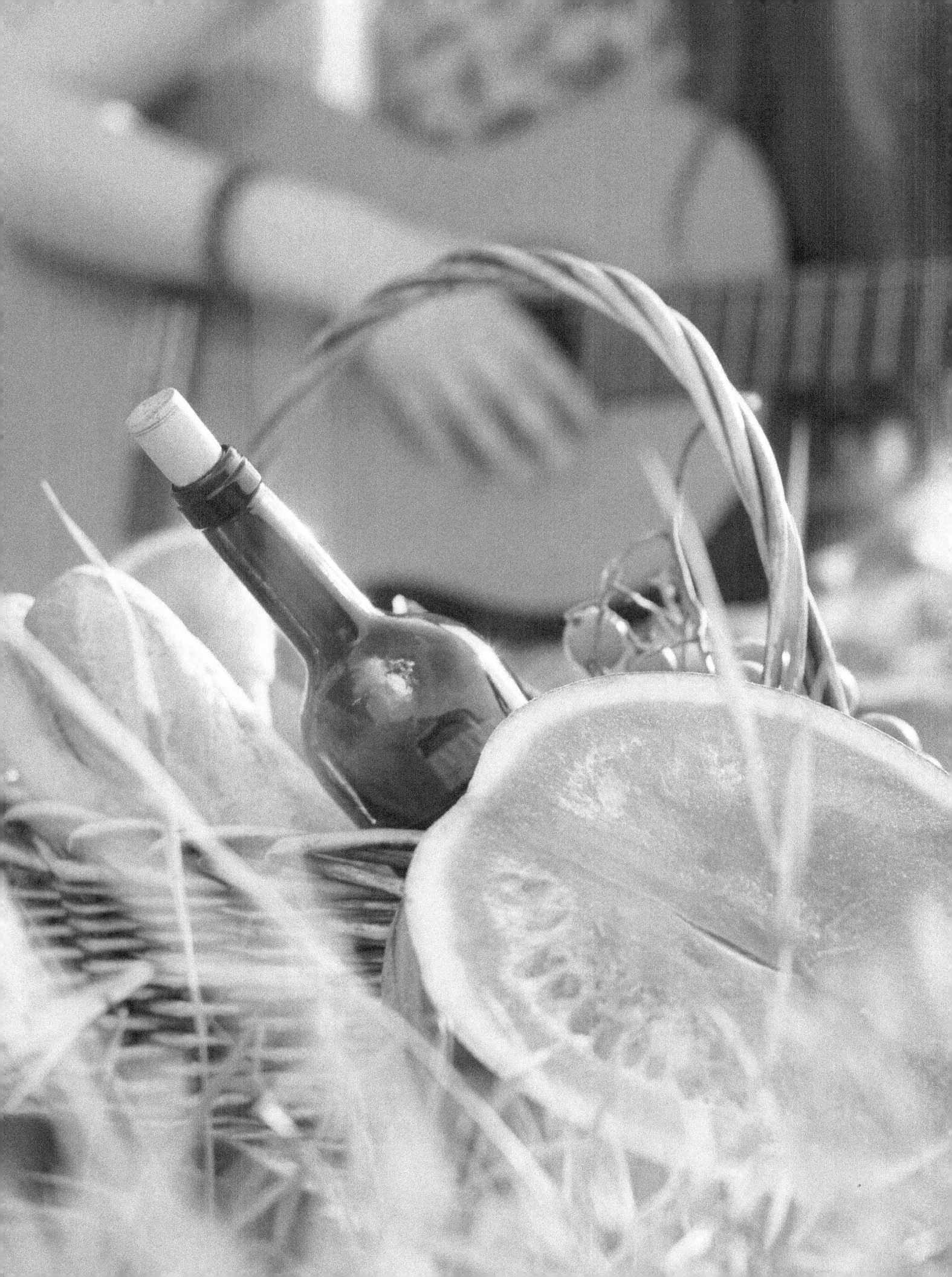

Materials Used:

Colored By:

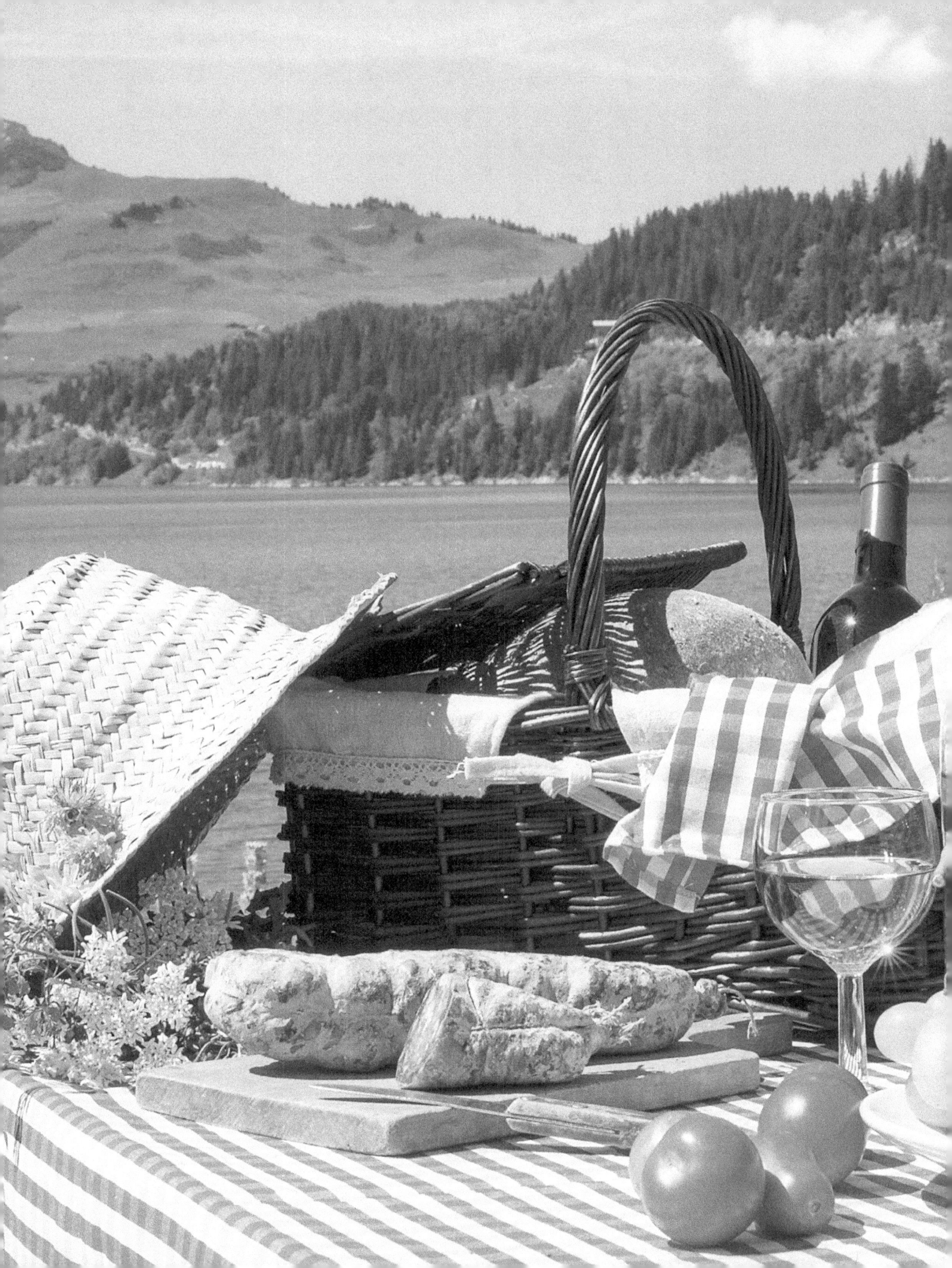

Materials Used:

Colored By:

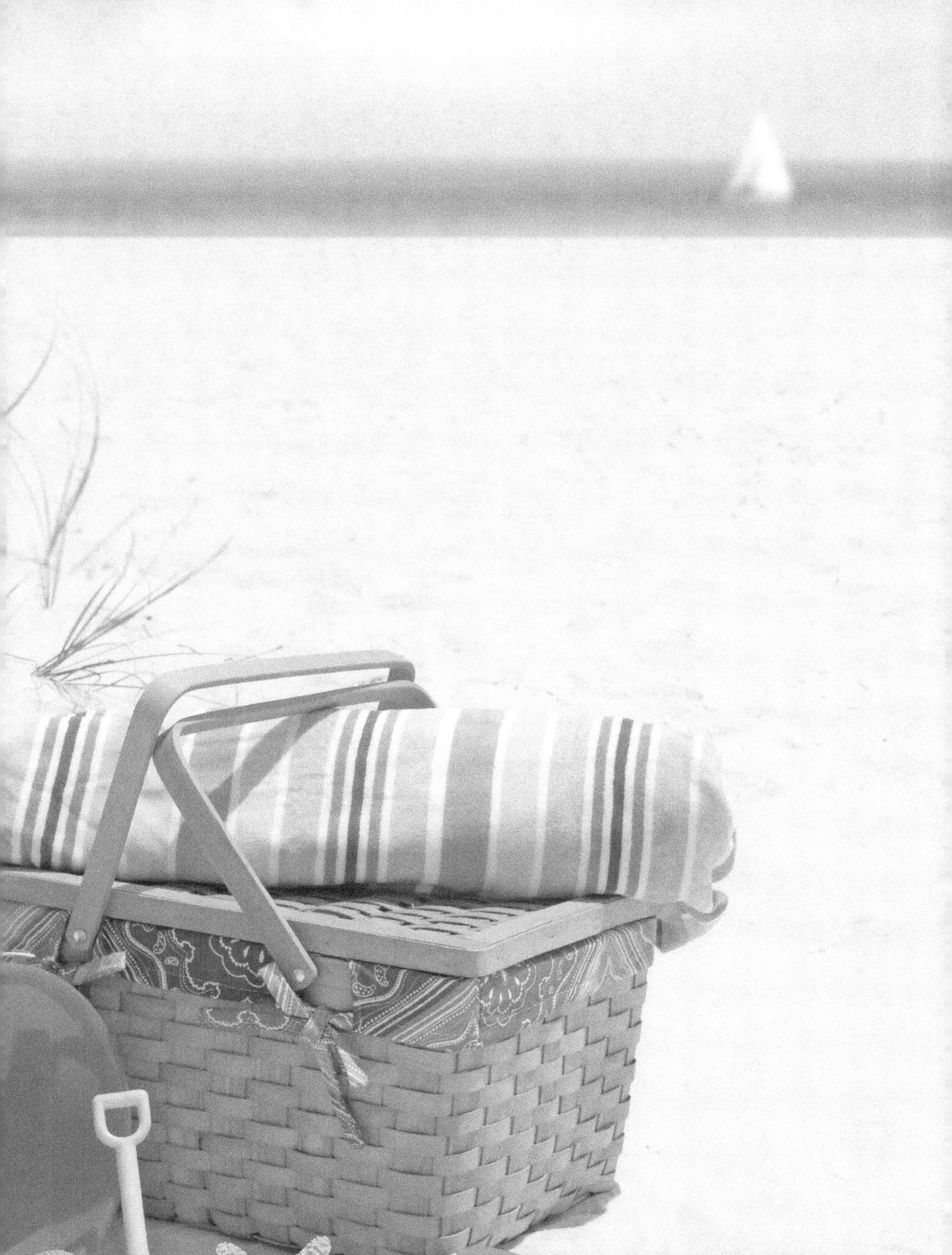

Materials Used:

Colored By:

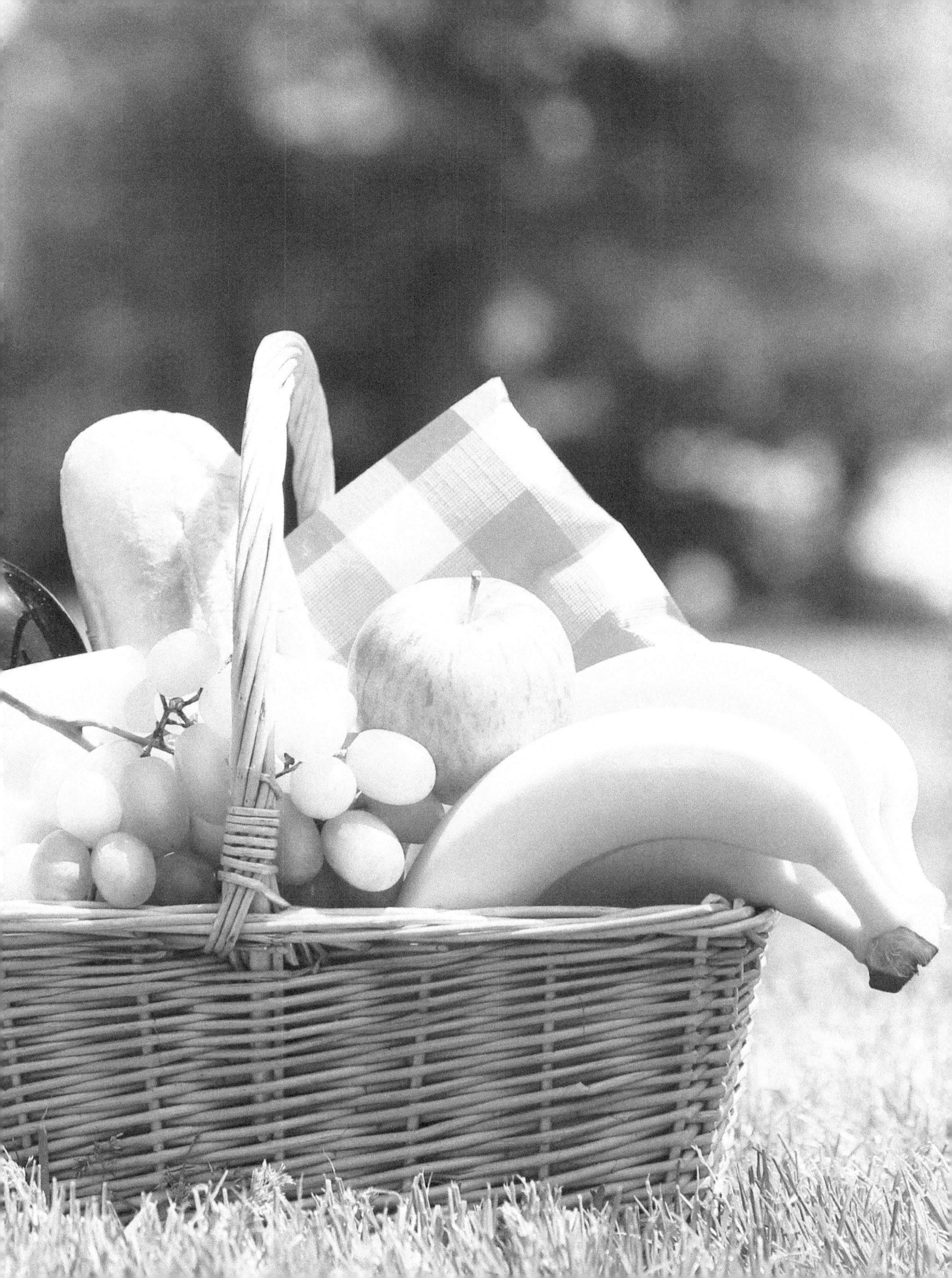

Materials Used:

Colored By:

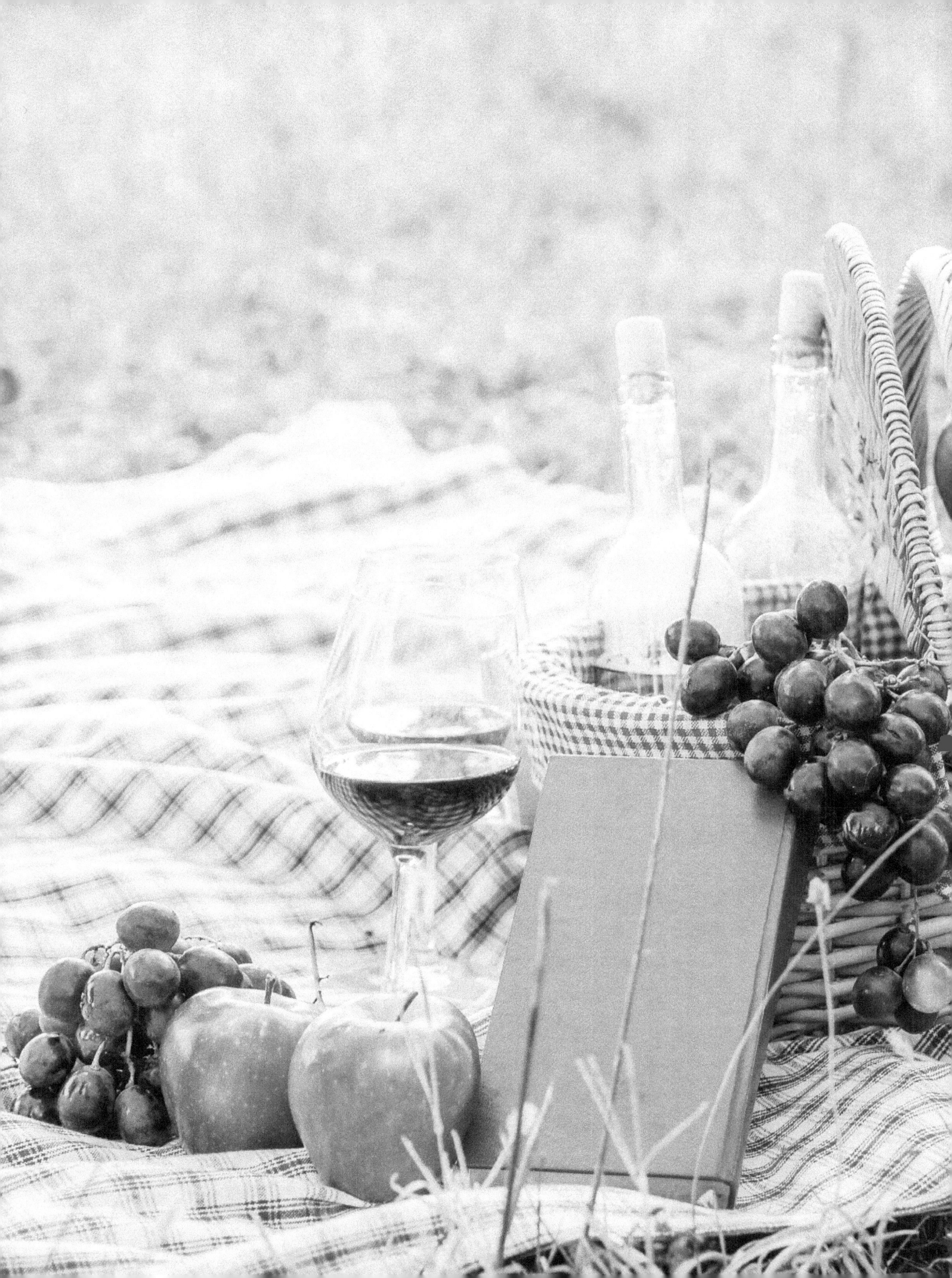

Materials Used:

Colored By:

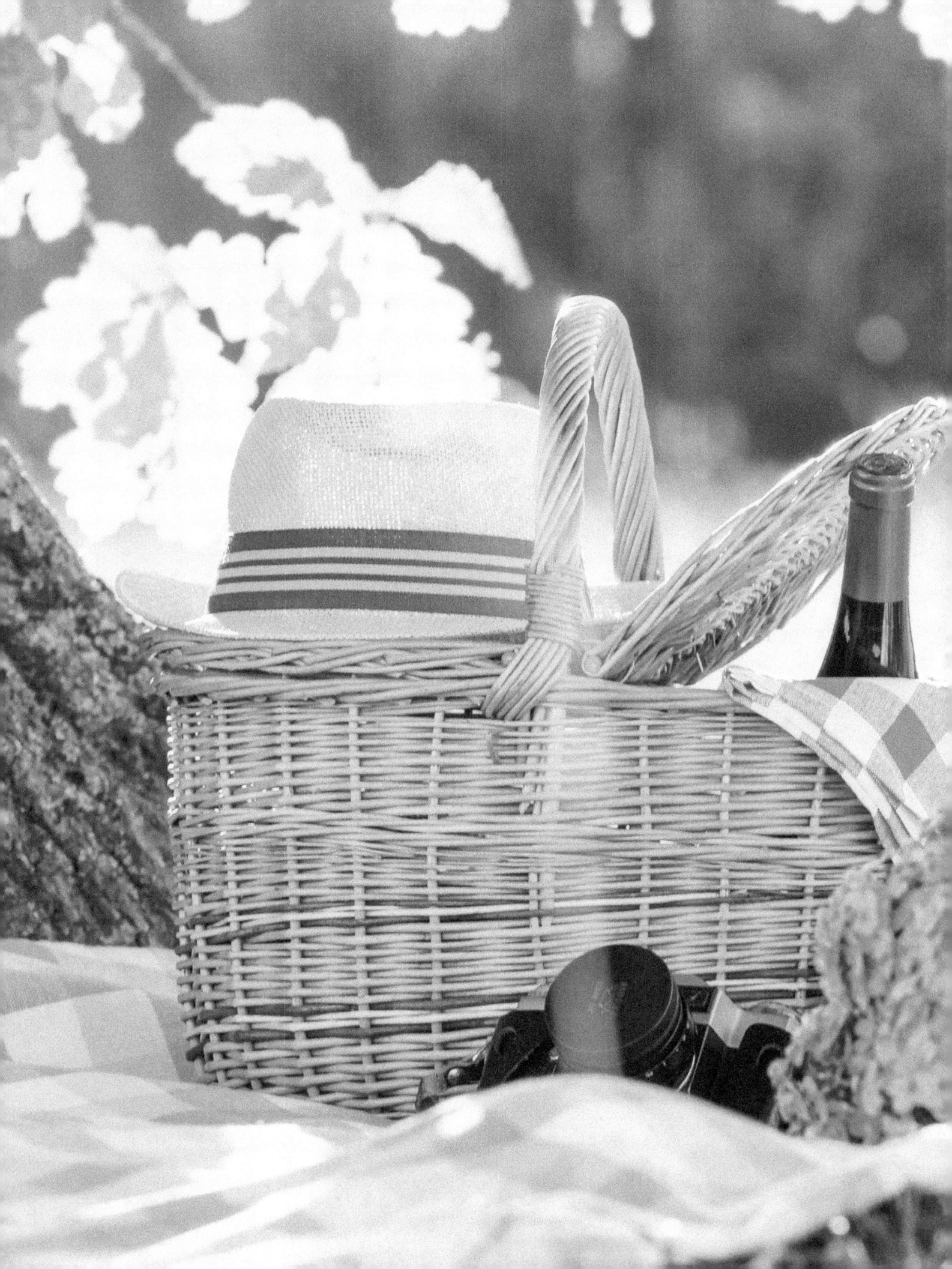

Materials Used:

Colored By:

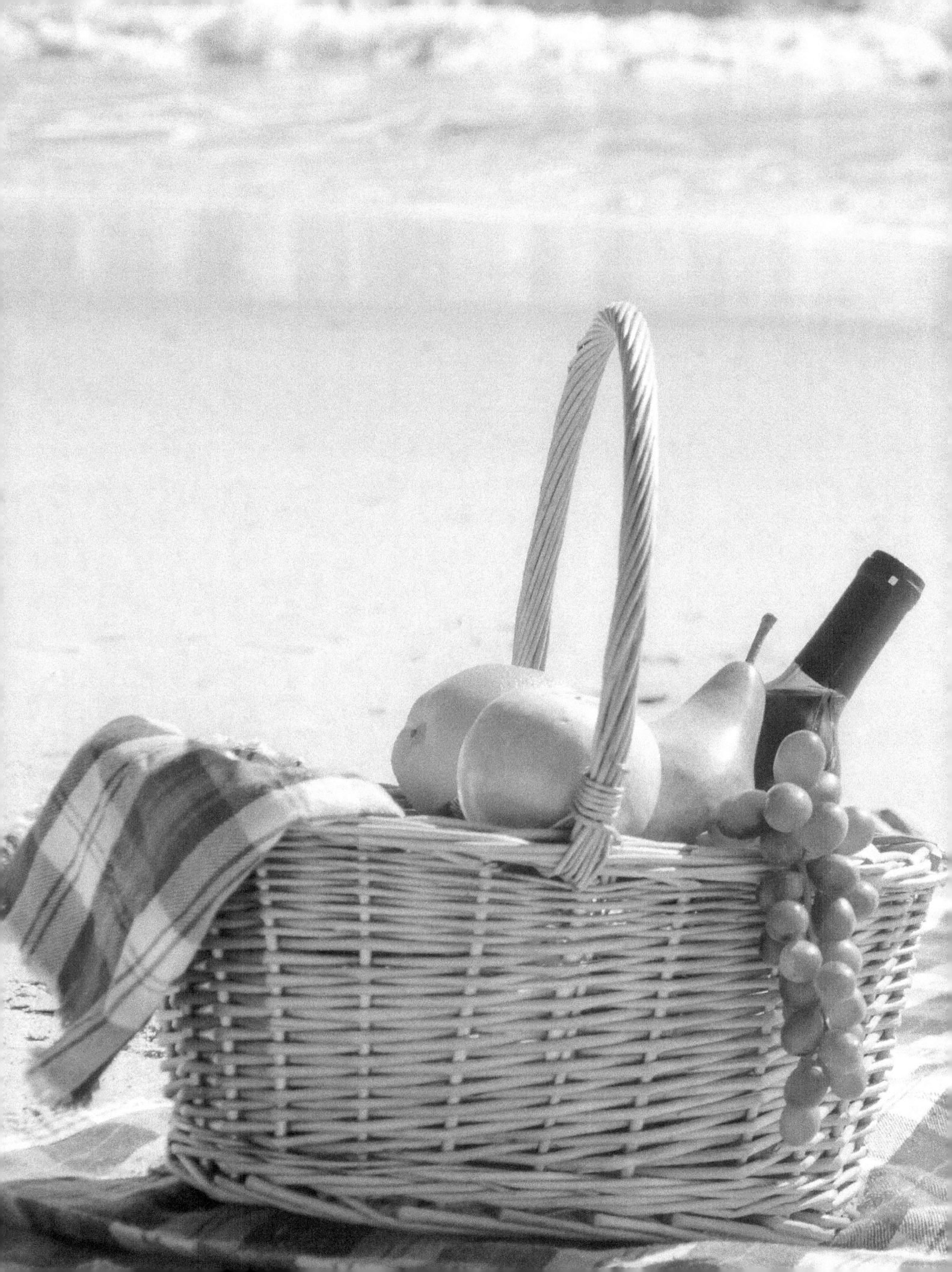